I know that I have not yet reached that goal, but there is one thing I always do. Forgetting the past and straining toward what is ahead, I keep trying to reach the goal and get the prize for which God called me through Christ to the life above.

PHILIPPIANS 3:13–14 NCV

THE 100
MOST IMPORTANT
BIBLE VERSES
FOR LEADERS

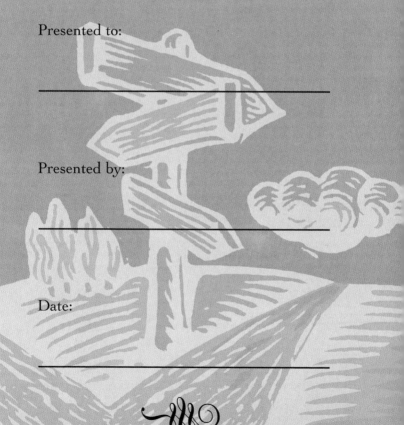

Presented to:

_____

Presented by:

_____

Date:

_____

Consider one another in order to stir up love and good works.

HEBREWS 10:24 NKJV

THE 100 MOST IMPORTANT BIBLE VERSES FOR LEADERS

W PUBLISHING GROUP
A Division of Thomas Nelson Publishers
Since 1798

www.wpublishinggroup.com

The 100 Most Important Bible Verses for Leaders
© 2006 by GRQ, Inc.
Brentwood, Tennessee

Published by W Publishing Group, a Division of Thomas Nelson, Inc., P.O. Box 141000, Nashville, Tennessee 37214.

Scripture quotations are taken from © The New Century Version® (NCV). Copyright © 1987, 1988, 1991 by Word Publishing, a Division of Thomas Nelson, Inc. Used by permission. All rights reserved. © The New King James Version® (NKJV), copyright © 1979, 1980, 1982, Thomas Nelson, Inc., Publishers. © New Living Translation (NLT), copyright © 1996 by Tyndale House Publishers, Inc., Wheaton, Ill. All rights reserved. © The Message (MSG), copyright © 1993, 1994, 1995, 1996, 2000, 2001, 2002. Used by permission of NavPress Publishing Group.

Managing Editor: Lila Empson
Associate Editor: Laura Kendall
Manuscript: Sheila Cornea
Design: Thatcher Design, Nashville, Tennessee

Library of Congress Cataloging-in-Publication Data
ISBN 0-8499-0033-6

Printed in China
06 07 08 09   9 8 7 6 5 4 3 2 1

Do to others what you would
want them to do to you.

LUKE 6:31 NCV

Contents

Jesus said, " 'Love the Lord your God with all your passion and prayer and intelligence.' This is the most important, the first on any list. But there is a second to set alongside it: 'Love others as well as you love yourself.' "

MATTHEW 22:37–39 MSG

Introduction

The Bible is the most conclusive leadership manual written. Contained within its pages is wisdom for every situation in your work and life. In *The 100 Most Important Bible Verses for Leaders*, you will find some of those most cherished truths from the greatest leadership book ever written. Each of the featured Bible verses was selected to help you accomplish what Jesus listed as the two most important responsibilities of a leader: to love God and to love others.

Every meditation in *The 100 Most Important Bible Verses for Leaders* highlights Scripture that provides the guidance and direction you need to be effective in your relationships with others. Along with an insightful discussion of the verse or verses, the accompanying meditation provides a challenge for you to incorporate into your day. As you embrace the truths of these verses, you will develop a greater understanding of God's love for you, your purpose in life, and your significance to others.

The Bible verses within *The 100 Most Important Bible Verses for Leaders* will stir your passion for God. These faith-building principles will help you nurture positive relationships with others and strengthen your influence in your organization. Whether you are emerging as a new leader or consider yourself an expert in your field, this faith-building book will provide encouragement and inspiration to you as you serve God through serving others.

You who are younger must follow your leaders. But all of you, leaders and followers alike, are to be down to earth with each other, for—God has had it with the proud, but takes delight in just plain people.

1 PETER 5:5 MSG

Be the Leader You Want to Follow

Some of the most loved presidents have been those described as "just plain people." They were approachable, genuine, real, and down-to-earth. Followers want a leader with whom they can relate, and who can relate to them. You may not be president of a nation or even a corporation, but because you have influence, it is important for you to be sincerely concerned for others while being yourself. The higher up you go in leadership, the easier it becomes to isolate yourself from the others whom you are leading. You may find it equally as challenging to associate with executives in the morning as with your children in the evening. By remaining authentic, you can face the challenges successfully.

Jesus Christ was the greatest of all leaders. He could have easily used his positional power and separated himself from others. Instead, he embraced people and even served his disciples by washing their feet in an act of humility as told in the Gospel of John. He was an authentic servant leader.

The irony in working with many different types of people is that as long as you are trying to fit in with the

> **By remaining authentic, you can face the challenges successfully.**

crowd, you will be disconnected from them. God has created you with a unique personality. When you honor him and yourself by being authentic, a natural connection with other people opens to you.

Examine your authenticity. When you act out of the natural personality and gifts God created in you, you will begin to feel at ease in your relationships . . . and so will others.

Wisdom that is from above is first pure, then peaceable, gentle, willing to yield, full of mercy and good fruits, without partiality and without hypocrisy.

JAMES 3:17 NKJV

Leadership Lifestyle

The higher you are in a position of leadership, the broader your influence will become on others and the more pervasive the responsibility will be on your life. When you accept the role of a leader, you accept the responsibility of influencing others. Maybe you did not realize you were signing up for a lifestyle when you agreed to lead the church committee or accepted the promotion at work. But leadership is not a job; it is a lifestyle.

Lifestyle leadership requires godly wisdom. Therefore, the wisdom described in James 3:17 is important for you because it presents a hierarchy or ladder of wise traits for the leader. Each characteristic builds upon the previous one and must be an integrated and true part of your lifestyle.

You cultivate a pure motive and character, which enables you to bring peace to others. You can then add peace with fairness to everyone in a situation. As you evolve as a wise leader, you will care for those in need and help meet their needs through your good deeds for them. As this display of wisdom becomes ingrained in

> **Leadership is not a job; it is a lifestyle.**

your lifestyle, you will become more unwavering and genuine in your leadership in every area of your life. Leadership is not a role that you play, but an expression of your wisdom to benefit others. The higher you climb in leadership, the less room you have for anonymity and conformity and the more room you have to influence others to greatness.

Make a list of ten people, including family, friends, and colleagues, whom you most influence regularly. Pray and ask God to show you how to be an even wiser influence on each person.

The eyes of the L<small>ORD</small> are in every place, keeping watch on the evil and the good.

P<small>ROVERBS</small> 15:3 <small>NKJV</small>

Hidden Cameras

Many days offer moments when you are sure that *Candid Camera* must be taping you. Some days things just go awry, or you may even be the one to go off-kilter. Leaders have their share of opportunities to make innocent mistakes, moral blunders, and ethical compromises. You may have privately experienced moments of decision or emotion that you would not want to share publicly.

Fortunately, every minute of the leader's day is not caught on tape to be scrutinized by others. However, there is a constant audience keeping watch on evil and good alike. So, how do you keep yourself accountable without placing every decision on display for others to judge? Remember that your most important audience is God. He watches your misdeeds and mistakes for sure, but he sees them through a lens of mercy. The great news is that

> God sees you when you give a simple compliment to the sometimes-overlooked receptionist.

he doesn't limit his viewing to the embarrassing scenes that you would rather forget.

God is not a faultfinder. He is not watching, waiting only for a leader's indiscretion; he also watches for good. He sees you when you take a stand for righteousness. God sees you when you give a simple compliment to the sometimes-overlooked receptionist. He sees all the deeds that others in your organization may not be able to see. God sees all, and he is admiring your good works too.

~

You should review your bloopers and blunders each day. Look at the hidden camera recordings, viewing as God does with mercy. Correct your mistakes daily, and commend your successes also.

Those who built on the wall, and those who carried burdens, loaded themselves so that with one hand they worked at construction, and with the other held a weapon. Every one of the builders had his sword girded at his side as he built.

NEHEMIAH 4:17–18 NKJV

Two-Fisted Leadership

An effective leader spurs progress. But you must understand that progress brings change and change sometimes brings adversity. You can handle the distraction of adversity by following Nehemiah's example. Nehemiah was a leader with a mission to rebuild the wall of ancient Jerusalem, which would provide protection, privacy, and prosperity for his followers. But as with all leaders, Nehemiah faced adversaries. His adversity came from both the outside competition and his own people inside.

Nehemiah's is an ideal and important example for you because he faced mockery, ridicule, doubt, even physical threats against his mission. By example, Nehemiah tells the leader how to handle adversity—work two-fisted. With a brick in one hand, Nehemiah continued to build the wall and equipped his team to build with him. He continued with forward progress while he addressed the challengers. In the other hand, he held a weapon. Now, as a leader you might not liter-

> **Equip and empower your team to build success in the face of adversity.**

ally hold a weapon today, but you can be prepared and equipped for the battle. Nehemiah did not ignore the insults or naively underestimate the adversary. He did realize the seriousness of the battle and stayed in a protective and defensive stance.

As a leader, you can follow this example. When you know that a change is inevitable or needed, use two-fisted leadership. Equip and empower your team to build success in the face of adversity. Establish your purpose, present your plan, and protect your process to accomplish your vision.

Examine today's biggest challenge. Write down what tools you will use to continue progress and what methods you will utilize to address challenges. Then keep moving in forward progress.

Get advice if you want your plans to work. If you go to war, get the advice of others.

PROVERBS 20:18 NCV

Safety in Numbers

Even the Lone Ranger had Tonto. Whether you are the top leader in your own organization or a homemaker leading your children, you endure difficult decisions with challenging choices. Often, even when you have prayed, listed your pros and cons, and given much thought to the matter, you are still lacking clear direction for your decision. You must remember that God hears every prayer. Sometimes he answers you directly, and sometimes he counsels through others' advice.

A leader is wise to develop a system of getting advice. You may form an advisory board, leadership team, accountability group, or circle of friends. Whatever you want to name it, you need a small group of trusted advisers who can share their wisdom with you in your decision-making process.

An effective GROUP of advisers offers: Godly wisdom, Realism, Optimism, Understanding, and Perseverance. Be sure to invite godly wisdom. God's truths are universal and have been proved successful. Advice should line up with the Word of God and be prayerfully given. A realist will give you a perspective of the good, the bad, and the ugly; whereas an optimist will give you the bright side of possi-

> **You need a small group of trusted advisors who can share their wisdom with you in your decision-making process.**

bilities. It is wise to keep a balance of both. With a strong understanding of your mission and vision, an adviser will help to keep you on the path you want to travel. Finally, your group should be persevering. A strong group of advisers provides the safety in numbers you need as a leader.

Examine how the five most influential people in your life fit into your GROUP. If some GROUP roles are missing, pray and ask God to direct you in relationships that will fill those voids.

Think of ways to encourage one another to outbursts of love and good deeds.

HEBREWS 10:24 NLT

Setting the Tone

Even though most people appreciate materialistic rewards, they are not satisfied with material perks or financial gain alone. Since Elton Mayo's Hawthorne Studies around 1930, leaders have understood that workers are more influenced by social demands, the need for recognition, and a sense of belonging than they are by raises and bonuses. You set the tone for the atmosphere that will meet the real needs of the people under your influence. You can learn how to create an atmosphere that will motivate people to achieve company or family goals while attaining personal fulfillment by encouraging acts of love and kindness among others.

The catalyst to attaining a satisfying and productive organization is encouraging your team to express care and compassion through words and actions. You need to think of ways to encourage this setting. It will not develop on its own, but must be intentional. Your list of strategies to set the tone might include a meditation or Scripture of the day, the celebration of birthdays and achievements, a company coffee club for breaks, special team lunches, family wellness plans, and flexible compensation time. The company newsletter, e-mail groups, team meetings, and family dinners are good avenues to disperse encouragement with little or no cost to the organization.

> **The catalyst to attaining a satisfying and productive organization is encouraging your team to express care and compassion through words and actions.**

Your initiative and intention in setting the tone will reap many rewards for your organization. When you strive to meet the personal needs of your followers, your organization will develop stronger unity and a more loyal and satisfied team.

Make a decision to unify your team. Then, establish a new tradition that provides an opportunity for your team to engage in conversation and compassion.

A good leader motivates, doesn't mislead, doesn't exploit.

PROVERBS 16:10 MSG

The Can-Do Attitude

Some stakes should be too high for employees and leaders alike. Often office politics offer manipulation and exploitation under the guise of networking and doing what it takes. In an exchange of "If you do this, then I will do that," manipulation may be the motivating force in managing results. You can "do what it takes" by remaining a positive influence in even the most political atmosphere.

Because of your integrity, it is imperative for you to embrace the fact that good leaders motivate; they don't mislead or exploit. Good leaders motivate positively and respectfully. Your job is to promote a motivating environment that not only yields profits, but also cultivates employee satisfaction and worth. Your encouragement and optimism will excite and energize others. A positive attitude is contagious.

> **Your job is to promote a motivating environment that not only yields profits, but also cultivates employee satisfaction and worth.**

Creating a can-do attitude is the key. You must first cultivate your own attitude within. Out of your own spirit, you can then motivate others to have an optimistic outlook. Catchphrases that have been used in schools and businesses alike are those such as: "If you can dream it, you can do it," "There is no *I* in team," and "If you believe it, you can achieve it." Even the three musketeers' "All for one and one for all" references the can-do attitude. By influencing others with your own positive attitude, you will cultivate a spirit of camaraderie that initiates achievement.

When it comes to leading people toward a can-do attitude, a pat on the back works a lot better than a kick in the pants.

With that kind of hope to excite us, nothing holds us back.

2 CORINTHIANS 3:12 MSG

Surplus Dreams

Do you live in the comfort zone of your capability, or do you dare to dream in your role as a leader? A leader's ability to have the biggest dreams of anyone in your organization is significant. When you plan, make it a three-pronged plan by setting a goal, marking a hope, and daring a dream.

Carry your goals all the way through to attaining your dreams. Goal setting is familiar to leaders. Goals should be attainable but challenging for your organization. Once you have set your goal, next mark your hope. What do you really hope you will achieve if everyone is working to his or her best capability? The final prong of planning is more daring. What do you dream? What is the impossible that you would be foolish to say aloud? When you know this is impossible in your own power and capability—you have arrived at exceeding, abundant thinking. God can do even more than that for you and through you.

> **Surplus planning almost guarantees success above and beyond your original goal.**

In your three-pronged planning, motivate your entire organization by sharing your goals, hopes, and dreams. Surplus planning almost guarantees success above and beyond your original goal. It raises the standard of excellence without burdening your followers (or yourself) with undue pressure. God is able to step into your organization and do the dream—even above what you can imagine or request.

Examine your organizational goals. Can you press them a little further? Take a daring approach and plan beyond your stated goal. Show exceeding, abundant thinking in your plan.

The LORD says, "Forget what happened before, and do not think about the past. Look at the new thing I am going to do. It is already happening. Don't you see it? I will make a road in the desert and rivers in the dry land."

ISAIAH 43:18–19 NCV

Caution: Bridge Under Construction

Change happens. In fact, change is one consistent characteristic of all progress. Think of the transportation system. At times roads need reconstruction because the asphalt has deteriorated and potholes have formed. Other roads need reconstruction because of economic growth that increases traffic and requires expansion of the roadways. A detour, bridge, or some other change agent will be required in the transition through the change—and even though there is hope for safer and faster travel, the drivers usually get frustrated in the process.

Whether propelled by failure or success, change is inevitable. You must be a change agent if you are going to be an effective and progressive leader. Change begins with a vision of something better. So often leaders have great vision for their organization and share the vision of progress with their followers, expecting everyone to jump on board, ready to enjoy the ride. As change agent, you should expect resistance among those who will be part of the change. But you have the exciting privilege of stirring enthusiasm for the new vision.

> You have the exciting privilege of stirring enthusiasm for the new vision.

Focusing on the "new thing," you lay out the plan for addressing change. You are the change agent—the temporary road or detour that moves people from the old system to the new one. You can relieve the sense of anxiety, create a sense of possibility, and instill an attitude of adventure among the people involved in the change by sharing a vision of something greater to come.

If you have a process that is not working well in your organization, envision a better way. Write down the vision. Make a plan to communicate the vision and construct the change.

Υour beauty should come from within you—the beauty of a gentle and quiet spirit that will never be destroyed and is very precious to God.

1 Peter 3:4 ncv

Invisible Vogue

As you prepare to enter the most important presentation of the week, you check the mirror. You find that your newest Hugo Boss tie or St. John suit looks as sharp as it did in the magazine. With meticulous hair, manicured nails, and perfectly whitened teeth, you acknowledge that you will make a perfect first impression.

You need to make a positive impression on others, so it is easy to get caught up in the newest look or hottest label of cutting-edge fashion. Unfortunately, that perfect look isn't permanent. The clothes will wear, the hair will gray, the nails will break, and the teeth will stain again. Maintaining the look of a leader is more about cultivating character than charisma.

> **Maintaining the look of a leader is more about cultivating character than charisma.**

It is important for you to cultivate true beauty that never fades. One might expect a leader to be described as a "mover and shaker," rather than "gentle and quiet in spirit." Insight reveals "gentle" as a type of reliance on God to defend your injustices, and "quiet" as being steadfast in spirit. When you become confident enough to know that you do not have to defend every decision, and you are secure with your own God-given abilities, you exude the beauty of character that radiates from within and is precious to God. Take as much time cultivating inner beauty as you do creating outer beauty, and you will make a positive and lasting first impression not only on many, but on God as well.

~

Conduct a character checkup today. If there is an area in which you are not relying on God to resolve a situation, pray and commit it to him.

Words kill, words give life; they're either poison or fruit—you choose.

PROVERBS 18:21 MSG

Sticks and Stones

"Sticks and stones may break my bones, but words will never hurt me." If you remember this nursery rhyme, you probably also remember the words to which you were responding. In fact, even children know that words do hurt. Often you realize the importance of words when you are the victim of a hurtful comment, even as an adult. Seldom do you realize how hurtful words are when you are the one speaking them.

You must realize that your words are powerful and carry great influence. Words can give life or kill it. You have a choice. With your words, you can stifle effectiveness in your organization. Or you can inspire momentum, impart courage, and instill hope. If a once-loyal partner leaves your organization, choose to impart hope for new opportunities. If someone makes a risky decision that fails, choose to comfort him and encourage his continued innovation.

> **With your words you can stifle effectiveness in your organization. Or you can inspire momentum, impart courage, and instill hope.**

Words have consequences, and you must accept those consequences. Begin your conversation with the end result in mind. You must choose what you want to cultivate in your relationship. You will reap what you sow, even through your speaking. So, speak life and reap life. Give encouragement; receive encouragement. Be a friend; find a friend. In choosing your response, you choose your consequence.

Give yourself three to five seconds to think before choosing your words. Then you will respond by choice and react by decision rather than impulse. Plant words of life and reap rapport and relationship.

In every work that he began in the service of the house of God, in the law and in the commandment, to seek his God, he did it with all his heart. So he prospered.

2 Chronicles 31:21 NKJV

Stellar Effort

You can be committed to many things. You may be committed to being successful, achieving goals, building a reputation, serving customers, producing quality products—the list is exhaustive. There is one area in particular that you must be committed to as well. You must be mindful of serving God. Working hard, generating profit, and demonstrating net growth are not enough. Seeking to please God is what it takes to be prosperous. The truth found in 2 Chronicles 31:21 is important because it establishes the precedent for prosperity—an advantage every leader desires to achieve. To become truly prosperous, you must seek God and serve others.

Your efforts must be excellent in serving God's purposes. You can achieve this even if your organization is not a ministry. Carefully honor God personally and professionally by serving others. You are his representative of grace and compassion to those around you.

> **Seeking to please God is what it takes to be prosperous.**

If you seek to please God with all your heart, then you will prosper. You please God when you serve others on his behalf. Your people profit personally when your organization prospers not only monetarily, but spiritually, socially, and educationally. Making a stellar effort can be as simple as writing a note of encouragement, sharing a meaningful Scripture, or lending a helping hand. The bottom line really is prosperity for others.

Identify someone in your organization who has had a difficult week. Decide how you can help him prosper spiritually or socially today. Then serve God by serving him.

Words kill, words give life;
they're either poison or fruit—
you choose.

PROVERBS 18:21 MSG

Let your conversation be gracious and effective so that you will have the right answer for everyone.

COLOSSIANS 4:6 NLT

Seasoned to Taste

You can be ready to answer others with communication that is full of flavor if you are mindful to season your words. Much like food, your words alone may provide the substance needed. But sometimes you can make your words more palatable by the extra flavors you add to them. A leader can preserve hope, purify motives, and promote integrity through seasoned communication.

A favorite seasoning for almost any meal is salt. Of course it adds flavor to a dish, but it also has many other uses. Salt is used in canning to preserve freshness and life. It also purifies one of the world's most precious resources, water. In addition to its cooking properties, salt can melt ice and snow. In ancient times, mothers even rubbed salt onto babies' skin to toughen it against bruising.

> **Your words can melt hardened minds and hearts if you choose them carefully.**

When you need to console someone who has experienced great loss or when you must confront an issue with a colleague, you may find yourself speechless, wanting to say just the right thing in the right way. When you aren't sure of the answer, think of salting your speech. Choose words that give life and hope. Choose words that are truthful and honest. Your words can melt hardened minds and hearts if you choose them carefully. You can promote healing for others by what you say to them. The right answer is to communicate hope and truth that bring resolution.

—

Make it your goal for people to leave your presence feeling better about themselves or their situations than they did before you spoke with them.

A wicked man hardens his face, but as for the upright, he establishes his way.

PROVERBS 21:29 NKJV

Counterfeit Leaders

A fine line exists between confidence and arrogance. Confident leaders are self-assured enough to believe that they are competent in their abilities. Arrogant leaders are self-deceived enough to believe in their abilities alone. Of course, there are also counterfeit leaders who are just trying to fake it until they make it. Others will decide if they want to follow you based on their confidence in your ability to lead them, so your self-assurance is vital to your leadership.

If you cannot genuinely convince yourself, you will never convince them!

In his "looking glass theory," Charles Cooley explained that a person forms his or her self-perception from three sources: who others think you are, who you think you are, and who you think others think you are. If any of those perceptions are out of balance, you may develop an unrealistic ego, self-doubt, or paranoia. You also must

> **The confident leader is self-assured enough to believe that he is competent in his abilities.**

consider another perspective . . . who God says that you are. In the Scripture, you are called God's beloved, an oak of righteousness and a friend of God.

When you balance God's image of you with others' images of you, together with what you know of your abilities and strengths, you are better able to form a healthy confidence that compels others to follow you. You do not have to fake it until you make it. You can be sure of yourself, even when you aren't sure of the situation.

If you want to have committed followers, you must be a confident leader. To be the real deal, begin to see yourself with the potential that God sees in you.

Do not change yourselves to be like the people of this world, but be changed within by a new way of thinking. Then you will be able to decide what God wants for you; you will know what is good and pleasing to him and what is perfect.

ROMANS 12:2 NCV

It Isn't Brain Surgery

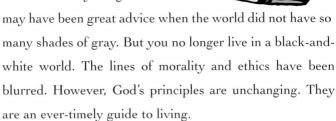

Your parents may have counseled you to let your conscience be your guide. That may have been great advice when the world did not have so many shades of gray. But you no longer live in a black-and-white world. The lines of morality and ethics have been blurred. However, God's principles are unchanging. They are an ever-timely guide to living.

Because your role is vital to your organization's values and ethics, your staff members take their cues from you. Your compromises become their compromises. Your boundaries impose their boundaries. So, from whom do you get your boundaries and cues? Ask God to guide you. Through prayer and Scripture, you can learn how to do what pleases him rather than what pleases people.

You must be driven by your internal, spiritual convictions and personal values. You cannot let external drivers force your internal choices. Sometimes being internally driven will mean standing alone in your conviction. Yours may be a single voice speaking out for justice. You might even be the only associate who refuses to pad your expense account.

> **Sometimes being internally driven will mean standing alone in your conviction.**

But if you are a leader with integrity, it is worth the stand. If you cave in to the comfort of commonness, you will cultivate a culture of compromise. If you emphasize the expectation of ethics, you will encourage an environment of excellence. Learning to be internally driven can be challenging; but it is not brain surgery, just a new way of thinking.

To be internally driven, you must know your own personal values. After prayerful consideration, list your top three to five personal values that you will be absolutely unwilling to compromise. Review your values daily.

Being afraid of people can get you into trouble, but if you trust the LORD, you will be safe.

PROVERBS 29:25 NCV

Leadership Paralysis

Have you ever felt stuck? You know, stuck, when you find yourself wedged between a rock and a hard place, where you are doomed if you do and doomed if you don't? If you have not yet been stuck, be assured—every leader will arrive at this place of decision paralysis. Immobility sets in because of your need of approval from other people. Your desire to be liked by your peers looms in the back of your mind, stalling your decision or action. This motionless place is where you are unable to carry out your decisions or even make them for fear of what others will think.

No matter how tough a leader you are, you do not want to lose friends or make enemies. You don't want your integrity or ability questioned. However, God has given you an expansive vision for your organization. You have a global perspective beyond what your constituents may understand. When you are stuck, you must remain the strong leader and make the tough decisions in spite of what the human opinion poll may reveal.

> **God specifically promises that if you put your trust in him, he will protect you even when you are stuck.**

Thankfully, God specifically promises that if you put your trust in him, he will protect you even when you are stuck. The wisdom found in this particular proverb is especially important for the leader to remember, for if you seek to please God instead of your employees, customers, or peers in every decision, you can trust that God will protect your reputation and relationships, thereby enabling your effectiveness as a leader.

Leading by fear of others disables your efficacy in decision making, but focusing on faith in God enables your success in leading your organization to effectiveness.

Steep your life in God-reality, God-initiative, God-provisions. Don't worry about missing out. You'll find all your everyday human concerns will be met.

MATTHEW 6:33 MSG

God-Focus

Do you see the glass as half empty or half full? Do you find yourself worrying what you will do if you don't make your budget at the end of the month? Are you often needing more to feel secure? As a leader, you have responsibilities and realities that carry financial burdens. You realize that if you do not make sales happen, then payroll could be affected. You carry the burden of not only feeding your family but all your staff members' families, too. That reality can be worrisome. So, maintaining a God-focus is important to your peace of mind in the realities of leadership.

God-reality is faith. When you look at the glass, see that it is half full, but see the potential for even more. Know that God has provided for you, and believe that he is the source of all your needs. Look at what he has given to you in material resources and human resources with innovation. Think of the lemon. It is just a flavorful fruit. But with a little creativity, it is a resource for lemonade, lemon pie, lemon cake, lemon air freshener, even lemon cleansers.

> **Maintaining a God-focus is important to your peace of mind in the realities of leadership.**

True contentment comes when you focus your mind not only on furthering your own business success, but also on furthering God's initiatives. When you focus on God's methods and trust him to provide what you need for success, you do not have to concentrate on lack. You can be content with the resources that God provides to meet your needs.

God-provisions often come in common packages, but have significant possibilities. Think beyond what is in your hand, and expand your thinking to the reality of God-provision.

P repare yourself and arise, and speak to them all that I command you. Do not be dismayed before their faces, lest I dismay you before them.

JEREMIAH 1:17 NKJV

Let's Do This!

From reality shows to extreme sports, players are heard shouting, "Let's do this!" many times in the face of fearful tasks. As a leader, sometimes you, too, have to get yourself pumped up to confront the challenge before you. Jeremiah the prophet had the task of bringing bad news to God's people. In essence God told Jeremiah, "Let's do this!" God's directive to Jeremiah is important to you as a leader because it presents a three-step plan of action to confront leadership challenges. As the leader you must (1) ready your-self and arise, (2) prepare yourself with information, support, and a plan, and (3) take a stand of confidence to set the plan in motion.

No leader enjoys bringing a disappointing financial report to the boardroom or announcing the need for staff downsizing. However, you have to present the truth, even the unfavor-able news. Once you have prepared yourself with the facts of the situation

> **If you have a tough decision to make, then make it.**

and have formulated a plan of action, it is also your job as the leader to speak truthfully and courageously.

You cannot be apprehensive in your mission or shaken by fear in the face of your followers. You set the tone and level of confidence for the organization. If you have a tough decision to make, then make it. But make it with courage and confidence, or your leadership will be weakened in the pres-ence of others. No one wants to follow a wimpy leader, but everyone wants to follow a courageous one.

~)))©

A positive attitude, courageous spirit, and reliance on God will equip you to conquer difficult tasks in the challenge of leadership. Get ready, get up, and get going.

You shall select from all the people able men, such as fear God, men of truth, hating covetousness; and place such over them to be rulers . . . Then it will be that every great matter they shall bring to you, but every small matter they themselves shall judge. So it will be easier for you, for they will bear the burden with you.

EXODUS 18:21–22 NKJV

Share the Load

Leadership can be exhausting! It is not a sprint, but a marathon. If you want to be able to endure the challenge of leadership over the long haul, it is important for you to share the load of leadership. As your organization grows and your responsibility greatens, you must sharpen your ability to delegate.

Delegation has a mutual benefit—it both relieves the leader and empowers staff. You must have a plan. Choose wisely those with whom you share authority, and issue responsibility according to the person's ability to carry out that responsibility.

You can start sharing the load by assessing where your organization is in the scale of management control and workplace freedom. Then, you create empowerment opportunities by finding areas that someone else can cover with at least 80 percent of your effectiveness. Once you find the areas in which you can share, you must choose the people to whom you will delegate. You assign responsibilities according to staff members' capabilities and skill levels. Some staff members may need to be given specific and direct instructions before acting, while others may be able to work with a global idea and few boundaries. Some may need to get your approval before going to the next step, while others may be able to act with initiative and simply keep you informed of progress. The key is being intentional in the delegation of assignments and degree of freedom given.

> **As your organization grows and your responsibility greatens, you must sharpen your ability to delegate.**

⟿⟡

When sharing the load of leadership, ask: "Is this decision being made at the lowest possible level?" If not, to whom can you delegate both the responsibility and the authority?

I know that I have not yet reached that goal, but there is one thing I always do. Forgetting the past and straining toward what is ahead, I keep trying to reach the goal and get the prize for which God called me through Christ to the life above.

PHILIPPIANS 3:13–14 NCV

Eye on the Prize

You have finally done it. You have been promising yourself that you are going to get into shape. Donning your new running suit and shoes, you set out on the track. Your plan is to jog to the one-mile marker and return. You don't want to overdo it the first day. As you approach your mark, you are feeling pretty good, so you continue forward. As you approach the second-mile mark, you realize how winded you are. Then, the biggest reality check occurs. You are past the halfway point. Whether you keep going forward or turn back, you have committed yourself to the full four miles! What were you thinking?

In your leadership role, you may have found yourself in a similar situation while running the course to attaining your dream. When you embark on the journey to fulfill the purpose you set out to accomplish, you have a passionate zeal to reach the goal. But at some point,

> **Your organization is counting on you. You are their running coach.**

sometimes at many points, you stop and monitor your progress. You may realize that the journey is longer, harder, and more tiring than you anticipated.

Your organization is counting on you. You are their running coach. If you sit down and give up, they will do the same. Applying the principle of "forgetting the past and straining toward what is ahead" can help you maintain your focus, allowing you to keep your team focused on the prize. Even if you know that you have not yet reached the goal, keep running.

Keep your eye on the prize. Do not look back at the starting line; it will only slow you down. Look toward the finish line.

Well-spoken words bring satisfaction;
well-done work has its own reward.

PROVERBS 12:14 MSG

A Handy Reward

Growing a business is like farming a garden. A good farmer knows that farming requires more than just planting a few seeds to harvest. First, he must determine what crop he wants to harvest and choose the right season to plant his crop. Next, he must prepare the soil by tilling and nourishing it. Finally, he plants, fertilizes, and waters the seed. The farmer must patiently wait and carefully check the plants' growth and production before anything can be harvested.

Like a farmer, you must determine what result you want to achieve. You must also consider timing as you prepare the people to receive your message by cultivating curiosity and engaging interest. Just as the farmer plants his seed, you plant the goal or vision. You must patiently wait and carefully check the fruitfulness of your efforts as the leader. After a long process, the farmer and leader alike can harvest from all their diligence.

This proverb reminds you that hard work does pay off. You are probably the most diligent employee in your company or volunteer in your organization. Leaders usually are. Sometimes you need to stop and remind yourself that your work should focus on the

> **Leadership requires the diligent spirit of a farmer.**

harvest you want to reap, not simply the work itself. Encourage yourself that the harvest will come when you diligently prepare the field and nurture the crop. Leadership requires the diligent spirit of a farmer. When you are diligent in planting and waiting, you will reap according to the work of your hands.

Review your calendar for this week. Are you spending time both planting and harvesting? If not, schedule time to plant some new ideas for growth, or harvest results by completing an item in your calendar.

He has shown you, O man, what is good; and what does the LORD require of you but to do justly, to love mercy, and to walk humbly with your God?

MICAH 6:8 NKJV

What to Do When You Don't Know What to Do

Everyone is waiting for your decision. You are stumped. You don't have a clue what to do. You have made the pros and cons list, examined your strengths and weaknesses, asked your advisers, and even polled your leadership team, to no avail. You may have even fasted and prayed. Still, you have no clear direction on what decision to make. What do you do?

Sometimes you find yourself in this predicament. When you are trying to make the greater of two good choices, or maybe the better of two bad choices, it is important to remember the guiding principles of justice, mercy, and humility. These principles can become a checklist for your decision. If you are humbly and mercifully making a just decision, you are probably headed in the right direction.

In your position, you have to prioritize funds, attention, and opportunity. You cannot always treat everyone equally in doing this. When you know that you cannot do what seems fair to everyone, remember to do what is just—honest, right, and equitable. Notice the Scripture doesn't simply state that you should be merciful, but that you should love mercy. So, if you

> **When you know that you cannot do what seems fair to everyone, remember to do what is just— honest, right, and equitable.**

decide to withhold judgment that someone deserves, you should not do so begrudgingly, but willfully. Finally, you should strive to walk humbly with God. For if you act justly, love mercy, and walk humbly, you may not please everyone, but you will meet God's requirement of you.

─⟋⟍◯

When you are facing a difficult situation, consult your check-list: Are you impartial in this choice? Is it merciful? Is this choice made from a humble rather than a prideful attitude?

The first speech in a court case is always convincing—until the cross-examination starts!

PROVERBS 18:17 MSG

The Rest of the Story

Some people call it a gut feeling, while others may name it a sixth sense. Whatever its label, discernment is valuable to you, because many occasions for discernment arise in your week. For instance, you may be fully convinced of a marketing strategy presented, until you hear the second proposal. Sometimes when choosing between options, with all things considered and equal, you just have to decide based on your own intuition.

However, discernment is not impulsive decision making. When you are pressed for time in your day, you can make a decision too quickly simply because the opening argument is convincing. Part of the process of discerning the truth is listening to the rest of the story. It is important to hear all sides of a case before making decisions, especially when dealing with relationship issues. Whether you are mediating a dispute or negotiating a compromise, it is beneficial for you to allow both parties to explain their behaviors, desires, and motives.

> **It is important to hear all sides of a case before making decisions.**

Being thorough benefits you in several ways. First, your staff or customer feels valued because you cared enough to listen. Second, you may be able to get to a hidden cause rather than simply the symptoms of a problem. Third, you collect more information to make a confident decision. Others are looking to you for the answer—proper discovery will give you a keener discernment in providing those answers.

Your organization counts on your ability to be both just and wise in "calling the shots." Discernment is one of your most valuable tools in powerful decision making.

${G}$o and make followers of all people in the world. Baptize them in the name of the Father and the Son and the Holy Spirit. Teach them to obey everything that I have taught you, and I will be with you always, even until the end of this age.

MATTHEW 28:19–20 NCV

Executive Coaching

Jesus showed his great leadership ability in this statement. He first shared his vision with his leadership team. It is obvious that Jesus was sure of his mission. Then he told his team exactly what action he wanted them to take to accomplish it. He also instructed them to multiply their leadership influence. Finally, he reminded them of the importance of leaving a legacy. This is an important example for you because it provides key elements to coaching others to fulfill your organization's mission.

You have heard the proverb "Give a man a fish and he will eat for a day. Teach a man to fish and he will eat for a lifetime." But what if you teach a man to teach a team to fish? Not only could he eat for a lifetime, but he could open a fish market and make plenty of money while feeding a village! You can multiply your influence by coaching others to succeed.

Follow Jesus's example of making disciples. First share the vision by showing that you believe in others' abilities to carry out the mission. Teach them the tricks of the trade that you have learned. Give them specific instructions on how to persuade or influence others to join the vision. Then reassure them of your support and commitment to them.

> **You can multiply your influence by coaching others to succeed.**

Be as sure of your mission as Jesus was of his. Then, teach others to become teachers of your mission. You will multiply your influence and more greatly accomplish your purpose.

He has shown you, O man, what is good; and what does the LORD require of you but to do justly, to love mercy, and to walk humbly with your God?

MICAH 6:8 NKJV

It is not good to punish the innocent or to beat leaders for being honest.

PROVERBS 17:26 NCV

Reprieve of the Regulations

There are many leadership issues that must be dealt with through discipline. They range from the notoriously tardy associate to the person who tells inappropriate jokes. They can be as serious as sexual harassment or company theft. They can be as simple as a messy workspace or dressing inappropriately for a meeting. You do not have to search long to find a disciplinary issue to resolve.

Very few people enjoy confrontation. You may know that you need to "tighten up the ship," but it seems unfair to punish everyone for the problems of a few. You can bring about improvement by addressing specific situations with understanding when they happen. Also, address issues personally and individually. Taking advantage of teachable moments is an effective way to handle mistakes or inappropriate actions. For example, if you see that a volunteer is not filing paperwork correctly, it would be helpful for you to explain the reason for the system and show the correct way at that moment, rather

> **Taking advantage of teachable moments is an effective way to handle mistakes or inappropriate actions.**

than waiting until the next volunteer meeting to bring up the matter.

Most of the time, being proactive is better than being reactive. Keep in mind that your goal is resolution, not regulation. When you address issues personally and in a timely manner, you will institute a higher accountability for the individual needing to change, while maintaining integrity with the other associates. After all, discipline is not about punishment; it is about improvement.

⌐◊

Stop the memo madness! Too often leaders take the easy way out of confronting or disciplining issues by creating a new rule or sending a memo. Be a courageous leader. Don't hide behind a memo.

In Christ, there is no difference between Jew and Greek, slave and free person, male and female. You are all the same in Christ Jesus. You belong to Christ, so you are Abraham's descendants. You will inherit all of God's blessings because of the promise God made to Abraham.

GALATIANS 3:28–29 NCV

Equal Opportunity Deployment

Embracing diversity is inviting each person to contribute his or her unique intelligence, creativity, and passion for the common goal of creating a multifaceted reservoir of abilities. You have a kaleidoscope of talents and skills among those around you, whether it is a circle of friends, church community, family, or business. When you appreciate the various strengths of individuals, the whole group is strengthened.

To appreciate the strengths of others, you must provide an opportunity for them to utilize their abilities. Develop trust with a broader range of employees by providing opportunities for them to prove their capabilities. Before you assign a new project, search your staff for someone who can develop with the assignment. Cross training and peer training are great ways for you to make learning opportunities available to less-experienced staff members while utilizing experts as mentors.

> **To appreciate the strengths of others, you must provide an opportunity for them to utilize their abilities.**

Moms are often great at allowing older siblings to teach younger siblings. The same concept is effective with adults. The more you teach others, the more you learn.

Make an intentional effort to broaden diversity. Invite new friends to your child's next play date. Deploy the young in the good ol' boy system. Send the woman into the man's world. Allow the expert to challenge the rookie. Do not let professional or cultural norms dictate opportunities. A diverse team stimulates creativity and builds people socially and professionally.

~∭◎

Invite a diverse group of friends for coffee or dinner to discuss a project or just learn about one another. You may be surprised at the hidden talents of those around you.

By helping each other with your troubles, you truly obey the law of Christ.

GALATIANS 6:2 NCV

Hugs and Handshakes

Technology is great. It offers quick transfer of information, faster production processes, and immediate access to resources. However, reliance on technology has also brought with it dissociation from coworkers and customers. Technology lacks the human factor. For example, many school systems and large corporations now use automated services to receive call-ins from sick staff members. Although the system relieves the need for staff and is more efficient in handling the calls, there is no empathy expressed to the sick staff member.

With the luxury of e-mail, voice mail, and fax machines, workers can go for hours, even days, with no real contact with coworkers, customers, or even their bosses. But people still have the need for a sense of belonging and purpose that comes through human touch and conversation. So, what are you to do as a leader? Where is the balance? Helping others with their troubles is a prime opportunity not only to please God but also to meet people's needs.

Take advantage of the opportunity to connect with others. The power of a handshake, hug, or pat on the back can bring hope to a discouraged staff member. Although an e-mail note of encouragement is better than no comment at all, it still is not as powerful as a personal conversation. Have a face-to-face encounter when expressing encouragement.

> **Where is the balance? Helping others with their troubles is a prime opportunity not only to please God but also to meet people's needs.**

Show empathy with a personal touch. Congratulate successes. Make eye contact to connect with others. These actions create a sense of belonging and caring in a sometimes cold and isolated world.

—

Slow down. Notice people's expressions. Does someone seem extraordinarily cheerful? Ask them why. Do you notice someone's hurried and frazzled demeanor? Stop and extend a hand or a hug. You could make another person's day.

The Lord GOD gave me the ability to teach so that I know what to say to make the weak strong.

ISAIAH 50:4 NCV

The Cheerleader

The realization that your team is only as strong as its weakest member can help you in two ways. First of all, when you need to replace a team member, do not hire someone at the same level as the previous member. Instead, hire up. Make the replacement member one of the strongest team members by inviting individuals at least as highly effective as those currently on your team. When you continually hire up, what was once your strongest member will become your weakest team member. This process not only increases the team's collective strength, but also continually challenges individual team members to increase their personal contributions to the team.

Second, when you realize that your team is only as strong as its weakest member, you realize that you need to help strengthen each member of the team. A secret strategy for strengthening individual team members is individual encouragement.

If you are going to cheer your team on to success, first determine what encourages each one individually. Some people are motivated by acts of service, so it is meaningful (and an ideal teaching environment) when you pitch in and help them on a difficult day. Others

> **Each person is unique, but each person can be motivated.**

might more appreciate a simple "Thank you," appreciation card, or public affirmation. Still some might be motivated by knowing how they specifically contribute to the goal, whether it is their creativity, critical thinking, or sense of humor. Each person is unique, but each person can be motivated.

As you use teachable moments as opportunities to encourage each team member, you will build strength in the team member and in the team as a unit.

D**o you not know that those who run in a race all run, but one receives the prize? Run in such a way that you may obtain it.**

1 Corinthians 9:24 NKJV

Gold-Medal Leader

Often, the difference between the runner who wins and the runner who loses is the motivation of the runner. Trophies are not enough to motivate the tenacity needed for a 10K marathon. However, more intangible rewards, such as integrity, compassion, and courage, can be the fuel that keeps the runner in the race to win. An inner motivation must fuel the leader to run a winning race.

Without a goal, you have no reason to press toward what lies ahead. You can create goals for every area of your life, including family and spiritual goals. Equally as important as the goal is the real reward of achieving the goal. What you really want to gain from the experience is sometimes more than the superficial tangible prize. If your goal is to have the highest sales and win a cruise, decide what you really want out of that goal. It could be that you do not really want the prestige or honor of being the most productive sales

> Intangible rewards, such as integrity, compassion, and courage, can be the fuel that keeps the runner in the race to win.

associate, but that you want to spend time with your family vacationing on the cruise. So, the motivating fuel would be your love for your family.

In leadership and in life, the goal is to finish your race. The way that you run your race will determine if your run was worthy of obtaining your prize. Your faithfulness to God and your commitment to others will help you to achieve success in your race. Run your race to win.

Write three goals for this week. For each goal, list the character traits that you will need to move you toward achieving that goal. Target those traits and run your race.

Do to others what you would want them to do to you.

LUKE 6:31 NCV

The Golden Rule

What could be more embarrassing than being told that you have spinach in your teeth? Looking in the mirror at the end of a long day of important meetings and realizing that you had a green-stained smile all day and no one cared enough to tell you is humiliating. How you wish someone had said something. After all, you would have been kind enough to save someone else the same indignity. The golden rule seems simple enough. You have heard it since childhood. But have you ever considered what it is that you want others to "do unto you"? Until you have discovered what you want, you cannot deliver it to others.

Everyone seems to want his or her share of attention, approval, and opportunity from you. The needs of your followers can range from a quick five-minute conversation to guidance on personal issues that affect their pro-fessional behaviors. Often, you are aware of needs that even they do not know they have such as train-ing, correction, and motivation. The

> **Have you ever considered what it is that you want others to "do unto you"?**

simplicity of the golden rule provides the essential wisdom you need to fairly divide your attention and approach your delivery.

The wisdom is quite simple. Do for them what you would expect for yourself. This wisdom fits all situations. It can save others embarrassment, provide awareness, or demonstrate concern. If you will treat others the way you want to be treated, you will produce a mutual acceptance and respect that enhances your leadership relationships.

⸙

When you doubt whether or not you should address an issue, ask yourself if your comments and behavior toward them are what you would want them to demonstrate toward you.

God so loved the world that He gave His only begotten Son, that whoever believes in Him should not perish but have everlasting life.

JOHN 3:16 NKJV

Unconditional Love

You are often admonished to know what you believe in. You believe in hard work, stewardship, and integrity. Or maybe you believe in talent, fate, or luck. Knowing what you believe can help guide your path in life. But a question can be posed. In whom do you believe?

From early in life you are encouraged to believe in yourself. "Trust your instincts and appreciate your gifts," you have been told. You may have been reared to stand on your own two feet in independence. Self-awareness, capability, and confidence are indeed desirable qualities in a leader. However, trusting in your own abilities or potential will sustain you only temporarily with partial effectiveness. It is not enough to have faith in yourself alone.

Faith in God is not based on ability, work ethic, or achievement. It is an expression of trust that God in his sovereignty will enable you to succeed. John 3:16 explains that when you believe in him, you will have not only temporary benefits, but God's eternal life-giving power. He is the source of all knowledge, power, and life. In the daily challenges of leading others, you can trust that God will empower you to accomplish your desires. When you feel powerless to resolve a matter, realize that your capability comes not only from your skill; you have access to the real power source that created you. Trust in his ability instead of your own.

> **It is not enough to have faith in yourself alone.**

Think about five areas of your life in which you are trusting in God alone to provide an answer or direction for you. Pray in faith and believe that he is the source of provision.

Remember that I commanded you to be strong and brave. Don't be afraid, because the LORD your God will be with you everywhere you go.

JOSHUA 1:9 NCV

No Man Is an Island

Being Moses's successor in leadership must have been intimidating. Imagine knowing that your mission was to complete the job that even such a great leader as Moses could not accomplish. Joshua was reminded several times to be brave in the tasks ahead of him. Just the foreshadowing of future challenges within this advice would induce apprehension for most. Yet, Joshua did face his mission with courage and strength.

A natural impulse of people in frightening situations is to grab for someone close. Even automobiles have embraced this notion and can provide voice-activated rescue if you become lost or endangered. Somehow just the knowledge that there is someone else sharing in the frightening experience is comforting to those in fear. People seek comfort and courage by clinging to others. Leaders are not very different when

> **Be reminded that you can be bold and courageous because God is with you.**

an intimidating challenge appears. A natural impulse is to call out for someone or something that can bring comfort and dispel your feelings of fear.

If you are new to your position of leadership like Joshua, or if you are a seasoned leader facing a new adventure, your courage can be attacked by fear. In those times, be reminded that you can be bold and courageous because God is with you. You do not have to back down from a challenge or venture because you are intimidated. You do not have to face your fear alone. Grab onto God to capture courage and stand strong.

ᵔᵔᵔ

If there is a new undertaking that you have been delaying out of intimidation, share the idea with a colleague. When you have another's support, you may gain the confidence you need to conquer your fear.

Know your sheep by name; carefully attend to your flocks.

PROVERBS 27:23 MSG

"Norm!"

A classic sitcom showed a recurring scene each week in which a man would enter the restaurant and everyone in the place would yell out his name in greeting. The scene exemplified the familiar line in the theme song, "I want to go where everybody knows my name." Indeed, everyone does like to be known by name, as it is a form of intimacy and familiarity that expresses value and acceptance. God modeled this for you by telling Moses that he knew him by name in Exodus 33:17. But learning a name is just the first step in knowing a person. In the Gospel of Matthew, Jesus told the disciples that the hairs on their heads were numbered and known by God. He knew more than their names.

Using a person's name in conversation helps you to connect with him. One great way to keep track of information about a person is to keep a client card or simply write the tidbits on the back of someone's business card after you meet him. When you truly get to know those around you, you become intimately aware of their likes and dislikes, strengths and challenges, and burdens and celebrations. It is by knowing them that you can attend to their needs.

> **Using a person's name in conversation helps you to connect with him.**

Your objective is to move your relationship deeper in the various levels of communication from superficial to significant. Purposeful communication can enhance your fellowship and build your opportunities for meeting the needs of others.

Target two people with whom you have experienced only superficial conversation. Make it your goal to learn and remember one personal fact about each of them this week.

Ⱨow much better to get wisdom than gold! And to get understanding is to be chosen rather than silver.

Proverbs 16:16 nkjv

Money Isn't Everything

Money seems to be the bottom line for so many decisions in business and in families. The quality-versus-quantity debate is discussed between teenagers and their parents and among executive boards of manufacturing companies. At times you must make a decision between the potential of wealth and the opportunity of learning.

Chick-fil-A is an ideal example of this challenge. For sixty years, the company's founder, Truett Cathy, has kept a "never on Sunday" policy in place. The organization firmly believes that their employees should have an opportunity to enjoy family and worship on Sunday if they choose.

Although it has been suggested that the company is jeopard-
izing profits, Chick-fil-A is satisfied as the nation's second-
largest quick-service chicken restau-
rant chain reporting more than 1.7 bil-
lion dollars in 2004 system-wide sales.
Another area where Chick-fil-A has
been questioned concerning profit
possibilities is their franchise opportunities. The company is quite selective

> **At times you
> must make a
> decision between
> the potential of
> wealth and the
> opportunity of
> learning.**

in allowing franchises. Over the last year, they approved
fewer than one hundred applicants out of a pool of more than
ten thousand interested buyers. The company is confident
that maintaining their standards and values is more important
than attaining a higher bottom-line profit.

You may not be in a position to close your business on
Sunday, but you may have a choice of whether or not to work
on your day of worship. Consider the possibilities, come
up with alternatives, weigh your options, and make your
decision.

~||©

Opportunities to choose wisdom over wealth are all around.
Examine your recent choices between earning money and
gleaning insight. Be sure you are budgeting your life wisely.

$\mathbf{T}$wo people can accomplish more than twice as much as one; they get a better return for their labor. If one person falls, the other can reach out and help. But people who are alone when they fall are in real trouble.

ECCLESIASTES 4:9–10 NLT

I've Fallen, and I Can't Get Up!

God's math doesn't always seem to make sense. If two people work together, you would reason that twice the work could be accomplished. Since this is the Bible, the principle must be universal, and so it seems it is. A team brainstorming new ideas can formulate a more exhaustive and creative list than one person alone. Partners that conquer projects together can finish in a fraction of the time that one could finish the job. In manufacturing, assembly lines seem to multiply in production exponentially beyond the number of workers on the line.

Everyone has moments of falling. Some people fall behind in their workload. Others fall apart in difficult situations. Having a friend to help you in those times where a free fall is impending is not only comforting, but can also help you maintain your focus on being productive. When you have a friend beside you, he can help keep you from falling in the first place by supporting and encouraging you. Then, if you do begin to slip, he can catch you or help you back onto your feet.

> **Friendship is a reciprocal collaboration.**

The key to partnership accomplishment seems to be altruism: the willingness of one to reach out and help the other. God said in Proverbs 18:24 that if you want friends, you must show yourself friendly. Friendship is a reciprocal collaboration.

If you have a business partner or spouse, consider how mutual your assistance and encouragement are for each other. Reach out to him or her with a helping hand today.

There is one who scatters, yet increases more; and there is one who withholds more than is right, but it leads to poverty. The generous soul will be made rich, and he who waters will also be watered himself.

PROVERBS 11:24–25 NKJV

Rich Generosity

You give, yet you receive more. You are generous, yet you are made rich. The principle is puzzling. However, look at the number of organizations such as Shriners Hospitals, Ronald McDonald House Charities, and St. Jude's Children's Hospital that give away free services to children in need of serious help. They give generously of their services, but they receive abundantly from others to further fund their giving of more services to others. The principle works: generosity makes you rich.

Many people think of generosity as giving money. But generosity is making what you have to offer available to others, and that can be more than just money. Whatever you have in your hand can be offered. Florida had a record number of hurricanes tear through many counties within only a few weeks' time. Many homes and businesses were without

> You are generous, yet you are made rich. The principle is puzzling.

electricity, water, even rooftops. The amazing thing about the news reports was that instead of showing people looting those buildings, the majority reported that neighbors were sharing homes, generators, and water. When they compiled all that they had together, they all benefited from each person's contribution.

What you have to offer is of value to someone, whether it is as simple as water or as extravagant as a new car. As you find ways to become more generous, you can expect to be blessed too.

⸱⸱⸱

Others need what you have to offer. Whether your wealth lies in your expertise, creativity, or encouragement, extend a gracious offer to help others. Don't wait until someone is in a crisis to be generous.

How much better to get wisdom than gold! And to get understanding is to be chosen rather than silver.

PROVERBS 16:16 NKJV

Freely you have received, freely give.

MATTHEW 10:8 NKJV

Looking for Handouts

Giving is more than funding charitable causes. Giving is stewardship of your time, talents, and treasure to impact others. Your time is possibly your most valuable resource. Unlike other resources, it cannot be recycled, replenished, or recaptured. Once it is given, it is gone. Yet, even with such great worth, time is often overlooked as a worthwhile investment in giving. Consider spending time with a cherished colleague, a lonely acquaintance, or even an inquisitive new staff member.

Talent is another precious resource that can be freely given to benefit others. Talent is more than being artistically or musically inclined. Skills, abilities, and giftedness are all forms of talent. You may not be able to volunteer as the creative designer of the new project logo, but you may be quite adept at organizing a holiday party for the staff. View your natural abilities and skills as assets and share them with others.

> **Skills, abilities, and giftedness are all forms of talent.**

Jesus stated that where your treasure is, there your heart will be also. So your treasure is also important to share with others. Whether you are tithing to your local church, donating money to a homeless shelter, or buying gifts for underprivileged children, your treasure can be a significant source of encouragement to others. Be willing to give of yourself freely to others through your attention, your abilities, and your assets.

Set aside five minutes to list as many of your talents, skills, abilities, hobbies, and interests as you can. Then think of ways that you can share one of your assets with others.

Remember this in my favor, O my God.

Favor

You get to know others by learning their favorite things. You may discover their favorite foods, hobbies, books, or television programs. You may even have favorite friends that you prefer to spend time with. With those friends you may not mind asking for a favor. The word *favor* means "good things." You might give your spouse a list of ideas for your birthday gifts, but to ask God to show you favor? It almost sounds presumptuous.

God can be your closest friend though. Throughout the Scriptures, he gives you permission to ask for good things from him. Because of Christ, you can approach God and stand in his favor. He is ever-present in your life, waiting and wanting to respond with favor. You do not have to be invited to the right business luncheon to make a connection. You can link up to God through prayer. He has all the connections you need.

> **You can link up to God through prayer. He has all the connections you need.**

If you need to be noticed at a meeting, ask God to show you favor. If you need to sell more products, you can request God's assistance. God can open opportunities in unexpected ways for you. He can give you the wisdom, creativity, and innovation to make the right impressions. When you ask for God's favor, you may find that you get what you ask for from him.

⟶⫯⟍⊙

Journal a list of good things you would like for God to do in your life. Prayerfully consider each. Be ready to highlight the ways God extends his favor toward you in your journal.

Commit your work to the LORD, and then your plans will succeed.

PROVERBS 16:3 NLT

Take a Load Off

God's will for you to love, forgive, and encourage others is revealed in the Bible. But what about some of life's questions, such as whether or not you should accept a job offer? Life would be easy if you could simply turn to a Scripture and get a yes or no answer. In fact, the answers to many of life's questions can be found if you commit your work to God.

First of all, you should not work for your own interests, but for God's purposes. Your plans and achievements are not yours alone. You share them with God. You can trust him with them. Allow God to be glorified in your hard work. Plan your steps and set goals, but maintain a loose grip on them. Be willing to make adjustments as needed. Trust that in success or challenge, God is faithful and sovereign in your life.

> **Trust that in success or challenge, God is faithful and sovereign in your life.**

When you maintain a willingness to trust God with your dreams and commit your plans to him, he will help you align those dreams to his plan for you. Notice that he does not bend his will to your thoughts; rather, he molds your desires to his will. You can trust that your dreams and desires are God's will for you when you think from the conviction of your heart along with the reasoning of your mind.

⤳

List three of your biggest goals or dreams. Pray about each and commit it to God. Then make a flexible plan of action to accomplish each.

This Book of the Law shall not depart from your mouth, but you shall meditate in it day and night, that you may observe to do according to all that is written in it. For then you will make your way prosperous, and then you will have good success.

Joshua 1:8 NKJV

24/7

You have only so many hours in the week. You work more than forty hours; volunteer at church another ten; eat, sleep, and spend quality time with your family in the remainder. You seemingly do not have much time left, certainly not 24/7, to meditate on the Bible. Balancing life is challenging for many people. The truth is that by embracing the truths of the Bible, you actually can live more accordingly with God's plan, which breeds prosperity and success.

The solution to balancing life is the ability to multitask. You can employ many strategies for meditating on the Bible by integrating it into other tasks and areas of life. By listening to worship music while preparing for your day, you not only energize your spirit but learn the Bible too. Whether you carpool or catch the subway, you can listen to Scripture meditations by playing inspirational audiobooks during your commute.

> **You can employ many strategies for meditating on the Bible by integrating it into other tasks and areas of life.**

Sharing a family memory verse is another way to meditate on the Bible with your family. Often your children may be able to provide the verse from their church class or Bible school program. You can review the verse daily at breakfast and over dinner. Dinner talk can be a great time for informal devotions with your spouse or family. In business, you can put this into practice through your company newsletter, thought-of-the-day e-mail, or weekly staff meeting discussions.

Think creatively to find ways to incorporate your desire to learn the Bible into your other priorities in life. Determine at least one strategy and put it into practice this week.

Search me, O God, and know my heart; test me and know my thoughts.

PSALM 139:23 NLT

God's Stress Test

Cardiologists often use a stress test to reveal the condition of a patient's heart. The exam will indicate if enough oxygen is flowing to the heart. It can also predict whether potential risks of serious problems are present. The procedure of the stress test is for the patient to walk on a treadmill for several minutes. While on his stationary journey, the walker speeds his pace on a progressive incline as the doctor increases the demand for performance. The physically demanding test pushes the heart to a stress point to detect problems and weaknesses.

God sometimes gives a stress test too. Like a doctor, he examines your heart to reveal your weaknesses and surface potential illness. Often your heart can be tested by the challenging situations that anger you. When you are pushed to your limit of patience, your words can reveal the condition of your heart. Painful situations can also test your heart's strength. When you are hurt or betrayed, your willingness to forgive is an indicator of a healthy heart.

> God sometimes gives a stress test too. Like a doctor, he examines your heart to reveal your weaknesses and surface potential illness.

The purpose of a stress test is to examine the condition of the heart before any damage is done to it. The test reveals what corrections and preventive methods need to be put into place to maintain optimal health. Regular heart checkups, both physical and spiritual, can keep you in a strong condition to fulfill your purpose. So you should guard the condition of your heart.

Ask God to look deep into your heart. If you detect unforgiveness, stress, or anxiety, begin a wellness plan today. Seek ways to decrease your anxiety and increase your peace.

You will be innocent and without any wrong. You will be God's children without fault. But you are living with crooked and mean people all around you, among whom you shine like stars in the dark world. You offer the teaching that gives life.

Philippians 2:15–16 ncv

Shining Stars

An amazing thing about gazing at stars on a dark night is that the blanket of darkness does not cover the stars, but actually enhances the beauty of the brightness. The display proves that light is more powerful than darkness. Just as a candle disrupts the cloak of darkness in a room, you are to be the light that interrupts the darkness in another person's world.

Being a shining star carries the responsibility of offering light to those who are hopeless or heartless. By living a lifestyle of holiness, you offer the teaching that shines God's love for others to see. Holiness sounds intimidating to some people. But holiness is not the same as legalism, religion, or even conservatism. Holiness simply means that you are striving to live an uncompromising life that pleases God.

> **Holiness simply means that you are striving to live an uncompromising life that pleases God.**

When you allow God to use you by showing others consideration, you are offering life-giving principles to them. Express godly character by extending mercy when it is not expected or by offering a joyful response to a negative situation. Holiness isn't hard. It can be as simple as an expression of hope to someone facing a challenge in life. Being a shining star may not bring you personal gain or fame, but it will give others around you the life and hope that God offers to brighten their gloomy world.

Let your light shine. Share the credit for success, congratulate a colleague for winning a sale, or send an encouraging card to an ill coworker. Seek out ways to express God's love through your actions.

Good leaders cultivate honest speech;
they love advisors who tell them the truth.

PROVERBS 16:13 MSG

No Yes-Men
Needed

If honesty is the best policy, why are some people so afraid to tell (or hear) the truth? Many times the truth brings disagreement or even conflict. In an endeavor to keep peace, or at least avoid conflict, people sometimes also avoid the truth. But ignoring the truth does not change it. Pretending that all is well when trouble is brewing does not make all well. Instead, it causes distrust, frustration, or disaster. Even though confronting with truth may be difficult, all conflict is not bad.

Some conflict, such as disagreement on a project design, initiates discussion or debate that may produce creativity, innovation, passion, and challenge. Although conflict is present, it spurs you on to function more effectively. This type of functional conflict can even become a creative zone for your team. Your task in constructing a creative zone is to provide an environment in which people are free to discuss their ideas in a nonthreatening atmosphere. People will not speak openly and truthfully if

> A confident leader needs others to challenge his ideas, convictions, and methods so that fresh insight may be revealed.

they fear repercussions or retaliation. As people see you respect and consider their ideas, they are more likely to freely contribute their honest thoughts.

A confident leader doesn't need a bunch of other people always in agreement with him. Rather, a confident leader needs others to challenge his ideas, convictions, and methods so that fresh insight may be revealed. As your team embraces truth telling, you will gain the sincere feedback you need to be effective in leadership.

—⁂—

Target a procedure or policy that needs to change. Initiate a discussion and cultivate a little creative conflict to stir enthusiasm and imagination. Challenge the group to negotiate their ideas about the change.

"I say this because I know what I am planning for you," says the Lord. "I have good plans for you, not plans to hurt you. I will give you hope and a good future."

JEREMIAH 29:11 NCV

Prosperous Plan

Jeremiah shared encouragement with people who were being held captive in Babylon. They had been told that they would reside there for at least seventy years. These people could not see a happy ending from where they were standing as prisoners. They felt hopeless. But Jeremiah provided a different perspective for them to grasp.

Being in a difficult place does not seem that it would stimulate hope. But hope is a by-product of problems. Challenges produce patience; patience produces character; and character produces hope. A new military recruit may not enjoy every day of boot camp, but on graduation day the recruit appreciates the skill, endurance, and courage that the rigors of training refined. An office manager may not covet the training process of using new software, but when the processes are more effective and efficient, the manager appreciates the increased profits. For

Hope is a by-product of problems.

the recruit and manager alike, fleeting moments of doubt and discouragement can be replaced by confidence and enthusiasm when the result hoped for becomes evident.

God allows you to understand the value of blessings through your circumstances that take you on the journey to hope. So, when God promises hope, realize that it may come from an unexpected process. Have hope in God, believing that his heart is to do what is best for you. Hope will never disappoint because it remains optimistic. When God is the source of your hope, you can believe in a better future that prospers your efforts.

Identify a challenge. Instead of focusing on the difficulties of the challenge, reflect on the benefits of succeeding in the situation. Write your hope for the future and remain optimistic.

Let us try to do what makes peace and helps one another.

Romans 14:19 ncv

Pineapple Perspective

Especially in southern states, passersby recognize homes with displayed flags and stone monuments depicting pineapples as the symbol of hospitality. The southern tradition dates back to Colonial America. During that era, dinner parties were a main source of entertainment in the community. An exquisite host would display a pineapple as the central tabletop feature, as it was an exotic rarity. The pineapple became the icon of welcome and warmth that showed guests they were honored and loved.

You may not need to hold a pineapple dinner party, but you can show your hospitality to others in creative ways.

Whether someone is a guest in your home, your business, or a seminar, you can add the special touches that make him feel welcomed. One simple way to create a warm environment is to shake a hand or give a hug, make eye contact, and welcome each person by name. If you have a small meeting of four, this is simple, but in a seminar of hundreds, you might station people at the entry areas to greet your guests. Offering

> Whether someone is a guest in your home, your business, or a seminar, you can add the special touches that make him or her feel welcomed.

refreshments, providing conversation, and helping others connect by introductions are other ways to make people feel at ease.

The pineapple is not the only icon of hospitality. Jesus displayed a hospitable lifestyle of serving others. When you show your care for others in a way that serves them, you not only honor them, but you are following the example of Christ.

Assess the first impression that your office or workspace displays to visitors. Add a personal touch of special refreshments or unexpected decor to create a warm and inviting atmosphere to greet your guests.

I, also, try to please everybody in every way. I am not trying to do what is good for me but what is good for most people so they can be saved.

1 CORINTHIANS 10:33 NCV

Living Beyond Yourself

Influence is the power you have to affect other people's thinking or actions by your words and example. You do not have to be a top-level leader to have influence. Everyone has influence. Teachers influence students, pastors persuade congregants, even children affect their younger siblings' behavior.

Influence can be positive or negative. Like the Corinthians were encouraged to do, be aware of your influence and use it for the greater good rather than personal gain. When you realize your impact on others and consider that impact in your lifestyle, you become less self-serving because you are more outwardly focused. Living beyond yourself means that you concern yourself with the needs of others. Although you do not seek their approval, you at least consider the effect your behavior will have on them. As you base your own decisions and actions on building up other people, you help them develop into stronger people.

> **Influence can be positive or negative.**

People all around you are watching you. You may realize your influence on some of them, like your spouse, your children, or your coworkers. But often there are others who admire and learn from you at a distance. If you want to be a consistent positive influence on others, embrace the responsibility of what you do. This will not only meet your needs, but it will also be a good example for others to follow.

~*

List several people whom you influence. Consider what kind of impact you have had on them in the past. Think of ways to continue your positive effect in their lives.

Wise men and women are always learning, always listening for fresh insights.

PROVERBS 18:15 MSG

No Status Quo

Have you ever wondered how household products can seemingly be ever-new and -improved? It is as if they are constantly adding new fragrances, uses, and features to products that have been around for years. If the product itself has not changed, then the packaging is at least redesigned frequently. The idea of something being new and fresh is appealing to most people. It intrigues and compels people to try it out, whether it is a product, a theme park ride, or a new menu item at a favorite restaurant.

Wise leaders are always seeking new ideas and innovations. You can find them all around if you are curious enough. Focus groups are often used to test new products, from detergent to toys. But you can use focus groups in many other leadership situations, too.

> **Many times innovations are born out of complaints or problems.**

For instance, if you are ready to revamp a policy at work, call together a focus group to discuss a better way of doing it. You can include a variety of stakeholders, from leadership representatives to end users. The collective creative pool may reveal more than you could on your own.

Often just listening to people's opinions in general conversation can spark new ideas for you. Many times innovations are born out of complaints or problems and the desire to do well. If you are open-minded and willing to probe for insight, you can find new ideas that raise the standard beyond average.

~

Choose a complaint that you hear often. Think of several creative ways to solve the problem. You will challenge your creative thinking, and you may even find an innovation.

Mercy and truth preserve the king, and by lovingkindness he upholds his throne.

PROVERBS 20:28 NKJV

At the Core of the Leader

Most leaders agree that there is no one formula to successfully lead people. Leadership is situational because of so many contributing factors that must be calculated into the formula. Because different situations require varying methods, approaches, and perspectives, you must maintain a few nonnegotiable principles on which to base your leadership actions. Those principles become the core values of your decisions, processes, and influence. Integrity is displayed when your actions align with your espoused core values.

It has been said that if you are not willing to stand for something, then you are likely to fall for anything. Your core values are what you stand for when you are challenged or tempted to compromise. Mercy, truth, and lovingkindness are a great leader's sustaining core values. Other values that great leaders may embrace are honesty, compassion, servant-hood, excellence, courage, and respect.

Values are the backbone that holds you upright with integrity. You can discover your core values by reflecting on the qualities that you

> **Integrity is displayed when your actions align with your espoused core values.**

would most want to be used to describe you by those who know you well. Also, examine those intangible characteristics that you would be absolutely unwilling to compromise in any situation. Having a personal values statement can help you face challenging situations that do not have one right answer. For example, if your core values are courage, compassion, and humor, your value statement might be, "I will face challenges with courage, treat others with compassion, and embrace every day with humor."

—⟊⟊◎

Meditate on those character traits that are most important to you. As values surface, select three to five of them and incorporate them into a personal value statement.

Give me back the joy of your salvation. Keep me strong by giving me a willing spirit.

PSALM 51:12 NCV

Yahoo and *Giddyap*

Some days are just difficult. Try as you might, you just cannot get ahead in your to-do list. You try to enlist others to help, but find them unavailable or disinterested. In the midst of such challenges, your day can become mundane and weaken you to the point of surrender. At those times, you need to regain your strength by cultivating a willing spirit.

In the old western movies, the cowboys would often rally up excitement by swinging their hats in the air and shouting a boisterous "Yahoo" and "Giddyap" just before they headed out on the trail. Even if you do not have your own posse to rouse, you can motivate yourself with a declaration of enthusiasm. A simple shout of celebration can pump up your passion and renew your spirit even on a challenging day.

> A simple shout of celebration can pump up your passion and renew your spirit, even on a challenging day.

Celebration is a catalyst to regaining your joy. You can reclaim your strength by calling out to God and asking him for joy. Ask him to show you creative ways to rejoice in life. You can celebrate on a difficult day by throwing yourself a personal party at your coffee break. Celebrate the goodness of God by sharing how he has blessed you in a quick conversation with a friend. The more willing your spirit is to rejoice, the more strength and joy you will find in each day.

~♦♦♦~

Create a happy folder to contain notes, cards, and photos that you have received that make you smile. A brief review of the folder can start you on a joyful journey.

Good leaders abhor wrongdoing of all kinds; sound leadership has a moral foundation.

PROVERBS 16:12 MSG

Solid Ground

At times, you may use power and politics to accomplish your goals. Often you have to turn a losing battle into a win-win scenario. Sometimes you even have to acquiesce to decisions with which you disagree, or compromise on an issue about which you have strong convictions. In other words, you confront ethical dilemmas. To be sure that your behavior is regarded as ethical, it is helpful to consider certain accepted criteria for ethical practice.

Ethical decisions take into consideration the greater good. Consider which result will bring you closer to seeing the optimal satisfaction of all people involved in the organization. Although you may seldom be able to please everyone, considering the best decision for the whole group will meet the needs of the majority. Free speech, free consent, freedom of conscience, privacy, and due process are all rights that need to be considered for the individuals affected. Your behavior should respect the rules of justice by treating everyone equitably and fairly. And finally, your decisions should be scripturally guided. Be careful to distinguish between your own personal convictions, denominational doctrines, and scriptural principles.

> **Justice is proved through your actions.**

Hating wrongdoing is not enough. Having a moral foundation for your leadership is vital. Justice is proved through your actions. Although you may not always be able to treat everyone equally, strive to treat everyone justly. By applying the criteria for ethical behavior, you will build a more solid ground for your platform of leadership.

The next time you find yourself in an ethical dilemma, give yourself this acid test: Are your actions for the greater good? Are you respecting individuals? Is this fair? Is this scripturally sound?

The mark of a good leader is loyal followers; leadership is nothing without a following.

PROVERBS 14:28 MSG

Rearview Mirror

If you were going to take a caravan of travelers to an out-of-state destination, you would have to make many plans. You would make sure that everyone driving knew the destination. Of course you would provide the directions, maybe a map, even an itinerary for traveling. Then, you would engage your gears and embark on your journey. But your responsibility does not end when the cars start moving. A leader that drives with a front view only can see clearly where he is headed. But if a leader doesn't check the rearview mirror, he doesn't know when he has lost his caravan.

Sometimes in the eagerness of leadership you can take off at warp speed with a new idea or project. You follow the steps of casting the vision by describing where you are headed and what the goals of the mis- sion are. Then you communicate the vision to all the affected parties. You hold meetings, send notices, and talk it up until everyone understands the plan. But you must also keep the

> **If a leader doesn't check the rearview mirror, he doesn't know when he has lost his caravan.**

vision in front of the people. Once your project is under way, continue to check that everyone is headed in the right direc- tion, and continue to stir the enthusiasm for the project.

Check behind you once in a while, or you will not know if people are still following you. By keeping an eye on the rear view, you can detect if people need rest stops, coffee breaks, or assistance in accomplishing the vision.

Choose a current team project that you are planning. Establish predetermined checkpoints in the project timeline to see if you need to pause for refreshment or redirection for your team.

He who answers a matter before he hears it, it is folly and shame to him.

PROVERBS 18:13 NKJV

Saving Face

Bosses tell people what to do, but leaders guide people to action. Decision making, intuition, and foresight are all parts of effective leadership. But sometimes eagerness to make quick decisions or bring resolution can cause you to act impulsively or get too bossy. You should try to balance decisiveness with insight to prevent becoming a bossy boss.

The key to listening is to be attentive in the conversation. You might be able to multitask, but you probably cannot multifocus. If you are truly listening, you must be focused on the conversation. Sometimes people listen in order to respond. However, you need to listen to understand. Then you can respond effectively. Listening to the matter at hand not only gives you information that you need, it also allows you to understand underlying issues that go beyond the superficial facts.

You can prevent an embarrassing moment for yourself or others by listening to all the facts as well as the feelings before responding. Then you can offer well-thought-out answers and effective decisions. Give God room to speak to you while you are listening.

> **Give God room to speak to you while you are listening.**

He will give you hidden insight that others cannot provide. If you react too quickly, you may not hear the treasure of God's words speaking to you. With effective listening, the people around you will appreciate your attentiveness and wisdom while you gain understanding.

—

Stop, look, and listen when someone interrupts you for advice or answers. Stop what you are doing. Look him in the eyes. Listen to what he is saying. Then, respond.

You should teach people whom you can trust the things you and many others have heard me say. Then they will be able to teach others.

2 TIMOTHY 2:2 NCV

Multiply Your Effort

You endeavor to surround yourself with people who are emerging leaders. But knowing when leaders in training are ready to lead for themselves can be uncertain. The Bible explains that faithfulness and capability are two qualities that you should look for in future leaders.

As a head coach of a football team, you would place players in positions where they would have the most optimal effect for the team. Let's say there is one player who is faithful to practice. He runs each wind sprint with all he has because of his drive to be the best. He is faithful to the weight room because his desire is to be the center on the offensive line. The problem is that he weighs 138 pounds instead of the needed 280 pounds. He would not be a good fit for that position because he is not able, even though he is faithful. Meanwhile, there is another player who can throw the ball a country mile. He is lean and quick and certainly is able to be the quarterback. But he arrives late to

> **Your job is to help develop the missing quotient through mentoring of the leaders in training.**

practice and doesn't fully participate. He is able, but he is not faithful. Both of these players could develop into vital team members if they were coached to strengthen their weaknesses.

Your job is to help develop the missing quotient through mentoring of the leaders in training. By teaching them to be both faithful and able, you will develop their individual leadership capabilities as well as their collective effectiveness for your team.

—⁓

Assess those around you with leadership potential. Help them develop their faithfulness or capability to become successful leaders by mentoring them as their leadership coach.

Our high priest is able to understand our weaknesses. When he lived on earth, he was tempted in every way that we are, but he did not sin. Let us, then, feel very sure that we can come before God's throne where there is grace. There we can receive mercy and grace to help us when we need it.

HEBREWS 4:15–16 NCV

Help!

Leadership does not come with a handbook. Of course there are theories, plans, and suggestions, but when it comes down to it, you have to think on your feet. Unfortunately, in leadership every person who attempts it is bound to make mistakes at some point.

Admitting faults and weaknesses is humbling for most people. Sometimes you do not even reach out to others for

help because it would require an admission of your inade-
quacy. But be encouraged. When no one else can console you
or understand your pain, God can. Because Jesus Christ
lived a sinless life, it is often forgotten that he was tempted to
sin, challenged in his faith, and suffered physical pain. But as
you experience in your relationships
with others, he also endured the very
things that you face in life.

> **When no one else can console you or understand your pain, God can.**

When you need help because you
have made a mistake, seek assistance
from God. Although your blunder may reap undesirable consequences, you can find relief in God. He offers mercy and
grace. When you are simply discouraged or doubtful, you
can be assured that his grace is not earned but is a gift awaiting you when you need it. Your responsibility is to simply ask
God for help. He will answer.

Make a list of challenges or inadequacies with which you
need help right now. Prayerfully and specifically request that
God help you with each situation.

God does wonders that cannot be understood; he does so many miracles they cannot be counted.

JOB 5:9 NCV

Expect the Unexpected

Miracles and wonders prevail throughout the Bible. Jesus turned water into wine when they ran out at a wedding. When a hungry crowd was without food, he multiplied a small portion of fish and bread to feed them all. When people were running for their lives and needed an escape route, God parted the waters of the sea so that they could cross dry ground. But those were Bible stories. Is it possible that God still does phenomenal wonders today?

You may have heard about some modern-day miracles too. A missionary tells of a time when his car ran out of gas in a dangerous jungle. Since a puddle was nearby, he filled the tank with water, believing that God could make it work. The car arrived safely at its destination. Maybe that is too unbelievable. But certainly you have heard of the lost and alone young boy who was found alive and in good health after a four-day search. Such a remarkable survival in the Utah wilderness was against all odds. Such coincidences can surely be considered more than simple fate or chance.

> **Is it possible that God still does phenomenal wonders today?**

When you have faith, you can expect the unexpected. The Bible is not temporary; it is eternal. Just as Job explained the wondrous miracle-working power of God, you can expect it to happen today. When you begin looking for them, you will see the miracles around you.

Note at least one spectacular thing that has happened to you this week. Instead of calling it fate, give the credit to God for his divine intervention by sharing it with others.

Happy is the person whose sins are forgiven, whose wrongs are pardoned.

PSALM 32:1 NCV

Oops!

Mistakes are a part of life. Some are so small that consequences are unrecognized by others. Unfortunately, other mistakes are of grand proportion, affecting many other people. But sometimes you can be surprised to find that a mistake is a blessing in disguise.

The only way to guarantee no mistakes are made is to prohibit trying to accomplish anything. Even though no one likes to make a mistake, this is not a viable solution. Instead, controlling your reaction to your own mistakes and those of others can revolutionize your organizational environment. When you accept mistakes as a part of innovation, you allow others to liberate their creativity. In a risk-taking atmosphere, people are not afraid to try new discoveries, inventions, and ideas. Understanding that mistakes are not only tolerated but embraced can ease your stress and compel others' originality.

Without someone appreciating the value in mistakes, you would not have been able to ever use sticky notes, eat chocolate chip cookies, or drink sodas. All these products were actually mistakes. Post-it note adhesive was slated to be a tape adhesive; chocolate-chip cookies were sup-

> **Sometimes you can be surprised to find that a mistake is a blessing in disguise.**

posed to be chocolate cookies, but the chocolate didn't melt; and Coca-Cola first failed as a medicine. But each inventor saw the potential of another use for his or her product. Some of them did not discover the value of their product for years. You cannot mistake-proof your organization, but you can fail-proof it by allowing your team to become creative innovators through risk taking without fear of reproof.

~

Think of a mistake that you have made recently. Stretch your imagination to think of a creative or innovative way to recycle the idea or product.

In all the work you are doing, work the best you can. Work as if you were doing it for the Lord, not for people.

COLOSSIANS 3:23 NCV

Impressing the Boss

It has been said that you can please some of the people some of the time, but you can never please all the people all the time. Trying to do so will only bring you frustration and discouragement because you are striving to achieve the impossible.

Approval from other people is not enough to motivate you to continued success. Man's approval is not consistent. You may please Jim today, but he may disagree with your next decision. Such temporary gratification is fleeting. Also, approval from people is not significant eternally. While he was on earth, Jesus was less concerned about whether people liked him than he was about fulfilling his purpose. You cannot measure your success based on whether others are pleased by your decisions. You cannot even rely on how well you impress your boss. Instead, gauge your success by how well you complete the goals that God has inspired in you. Your motivation must be intrinsic and purposeful if it is to be sustaining.

> **Gauge your success by how well you complete the goals that God has inspired in you.**

Bill Cosby once stated, "I do not know the formula for success, but the way to failure is to try and please everyone." Your audience is not the crowd around you. Your most important audience is God. If you seek to please him in all that you do, he will persuade the onlookers. Find your motivation through satisfying God.

In the next tough decision that brings concern of what people will think about you, weigh the value of their opinions carefully. Then ask yourself if God will be pleased with you too.

I know your works. See, I have set before you an open door, and no one can shut it; for you have a little strength, have kept My word, and have not denied My name.

REVELATION 3:8 NKJV

Automatic Doors

Imagine that you have just completed conducting a day-long seminar. You have packed your materials, loaded your laptop, stacked your briefcases, and are scurrying out to catch your cab. You prepare to leave the building, holding one briefcase in hand and another under your arm, while pulling a cart with the other hand. As you arrive at the door you stop. *How am I going to push this door open without dropping everything?* You groan, finding no one to help you. How exhausting to manage your load and struggle to get the door open too. Those are the times when you hope for an automatic door—one that will just fly open as you move toward it, allowing you to exit with ease.

Now imagine that in the midst of your struggle God has set before you an automatic door. As you move toward it, the door just flies open with no effort from you. Why would he do that for you? He says that he will do it because he knows that you have little strength, and yet have obeyed his word and not denied his name.

> When you honor God by following his ways, he honors you by sharing his power.

Continue to imagine. What struggle leaves you with only a little strength? It is important to remember that you do not have the power to open some doors of opportunity; but God does. When you honor God by following his ways, he honors you by sharing his power, which opens doors with an automatic ease in ways you cannot.

Acknowledge God's name as the source of strength. Wait for the door to open automatically, divinely, using his strength instead of your own to move forward.

Come, let us go.

1 Samuel 14:1 NKJV

Saddle Up

Jonathan was the king's son. Like the other men in the army, he was to get his directions for battle from the king. But the king was afraid and so was his army. They all sat down under a pomegranate tree to consider their options for fighting the Philistines, who outnumbered them. But Jonathan had a notion. He and his assistant sneaked away from camp to survey the situation. He asked for God's direction in helping them identify a good opportunity to attack the enemy. When the moment arrived, Jonathan responded, "Come, let us go."

Jonathan was optimistic and opportunistic. He believed that with God's help, he could make a difference in the battle. He had a victor's attitude. But he did not react impulsively. He examined his situation and looked for the right opportunity. Then he seized the moment to succeed. God did help them win the battle. In fact, once his father the king saw the battle was under way, he led the troops to help fight.

> **You can take advantage of opportunities that others do not even see.**

You can take advantage of opportunities that others do not even see. When you look at the glass of water and see it as half empty, view it as an opportunity to add fresh water to the mix. If God can enable two young men to battle an army of thousands and win, he can help you to accomplish incredible feats in leadership.

~卅〇

Target an opportunity that has lain dormant. Pray for God to show you creative ways to take full advantage of its possibilities. Then take a step of action and implement one of the strategies.

I remind you to keep using the gift God gave you . . . let it grow, as a small flame grows into a fire.

2 TIMOTHY 1:6 NCV

Burning Desire

Good Boy Scouts know how to start fires. Although there are reports of using such strange items as a soda can or a chocolate bar, there are several common elements required to ignite any fire. You need something to create a spark, material to use as tinder to turn the spark into a flame, and kindling to generate a fire from the initial flame.

Igniting passion in yourself and others is much the same as starting a fire. God gave you what you need for the spark. He created you with the gifts found in your talents, skills, and abilities. Your responsibility is to take that spark and turn it into a flame. You can find the tinder of opportunities for using your gifts all around you. But using your gifts once in a lifetime or once in a while is not enough to maintain a fire. The flame must be continually kindled to keep the fire going. The more you put your gifts to work, the more you feed the flame within you.

> The more you put your gifts to work, the more you feed the flame within you.

Passion is that fire within. It is that burning desire to make a difference in the world around you. Passion can be more than a temporary excitement. As you fan the flame of the God-given spark within you, you can maintain zeal to achieve great accomplishments in life.

Check your fire. Does it need a little kindling to energize it? If so, put one of your gifts to work in a community service project and recapture your enthusiasm.

I remind you to keep using the gift God gave you . . . Let it grow, as a small flame grows into a fire.

2 TIMOTHY 1:6 NCV

Those who plan peace have joy.

PROVERBS 12:20 ESV

Purposeful Peace

You have the power to set others up for greatness. When coworkers share their aspirations with you, your words and actions regarding their dreams can be a conduit of inspiration. In a competitive world in which candidates are pitted against one another to receive promotions, people can become envious. Envy causes deceit and conceit toward others. But when you are self-confident and rely on God for all your promotions, you do not have to be intimidated by the success of others. You can encourage others and help them succeed, and at the same time be a winner yourself.

When you choose to take actions of peace, you build others up. You can help others achieve their dreams by equipping them with methods and motivation that will lead to success. If colleagues share new product or service ideas with you, help them brainstorm through the possible design and promotion ideas without expecting a return on your efforts. The knowledge that you had a part in the achievement and the success of others is itself a joyful reward.

> **The knowledge that you had a part in the achievement and the success of others is itself a joyful reward.**

Find ways to motivate your personal and professional peers. Be confident enough to let others use your expertise to achieve their own goals. Find enjoyment in the success of others by planning for their peace.

⚬

Ask a colleague to share his or her aspirations with you. Then ask how you can be supportive in achieving that goal. Be sure to encourage and empower your colleague along the way to success.

God began doing a good work in you, and I am sure he will continue it until it is finished when Jesus Christ comes again.

PHILIPPIANS 1:6 NCV

The Grand Finale

An evangelist tells of a time when she was traveling in the Midwest preaching in small churches. She drove through miles and miles of farmland. The scenery of corn, wheat, and bean fields became boring, and she became weary of the view. It seemed to be just a long trip of the same relentless sights over and over. But when she departed by plane and her view lifted to new heights, the dullness was replaced by a picturesque weave of colors and depth that was beautiful.

When you are working in the routine of your job and relationships, you cannot see the finished product. Sometimes what appear to you as redundant, maybe even meaningless tasks can actually be part of God's grand plan for you. A quilter can take remnants of fine linen and mix them with scraps of common cloth to create a beautiful patchwork of comfort and warmth. God can do the same with the events of your life. God

> God can mix your most heroic successes with your most humbling failures and make a significant ministry out of them.

can mix your most heroic successes with your most humbling failures and make a significant ministry out of them.

You have to persevere long enough to view the field from the sky and see the rags turned into the quilt to understand God's plan. You can trust that he had a plan for your life when he created you. If you are willing to be tenacious enough to make it to the end with him, he will complete his purpose for you.

Write your life mission or purpose in a ten-word statement. Read your mission statement at the beginning and ending of each day as a reminder of your purpose in life.

I can do all things through Christ who strengthens me.

PHILIPPIANS 4:13 NKJV

Gotta Make It

The Little Engine That Could is a story of persistence. The Little Engine was determined to make it to his destination. Although he ran across challenges, obstacles, and discouragement, he did not stop. He may have huffed his way to success as he chanted to himself that he could make it, but he did make it in the end. Sometimes you may feel like giving up or giving in. You may feel as if you are beating your head against the wall, that you are up against a brick wall, or maybe even that you are just exhausted. In whatever jargon you express it, you feel like quitting.

Persist. You can do it. You may have to sing, "gotta make it" or "I can do all things" along the way, but you can do it. What you cannot do is persist in your own strength. Philippians clearly explains that your strength must come through Christ. He is the One who can enable and empower you to do all things.

> **Your strength must come through Christ. He is the one who can enable and empower you to do all things.**

Keep moving forward even if you see others running out of steam or derailing. Sometimes the journey may be a steady, challenging incline or a full-speed, frightening descent, but you can enjoy the thrill of the ride. Rely on Christ for your strength, and you will make it to your destination.

Break your large project into smaller, more feasible benchmarks. Think of each mark as a rest stop to refuel with energy and passion. At each rest stop, ask God to join you on the journey.

Those who hear God's teaching and do nothing are like people who look at themselves in a mirror. They see their faces and then go away and quickly forget what they looked like. But the truly happy people are those who carefully study God's perfect law that makes people free, and they continue to study it.

JAMES 1:23–25 NCV

Who's the Fairest of Them All?

Quite a bit of attention is given to professional development. Continuous improvement in skills, procedures, and professionalism is emphasized in most organizations. Personal growth is sometimes assumed as part of vocational training, but personal growth is a field of its own. Identifying a technical skill to learn or improve may be easier than selecting a personal trait to develop. But you can target areas for self-improvement just as you can areas for professional growth.

One way to decide in what areas you want to improve is to study the Scripture. The Bible provides many sources of discovery, such as the proverbs about temperament and communication or the beatitudes regarding attitudes. For example, if you study the fruit of the Spirit, which includes love, joy, peace,

> **The Bible is full of ideas to examine for your potential life lessons.**

and patience, among others, you might find that you could improve in the area of patience. Once you have progressed well in patience, you can move to one of the other areas listed.

Once you target an area in which you want to grow, you simply make a plan. You might plan to learn some stress relievers or rehearse patience by choosing the longest line at the grocery store just for the practice. As in any professional area, you will find that you can make great strides in your personal growth by taking a sober look at your reflection in the mirror.

Target an area of personal growth to work on. Write down your goals and steps for improvement. Put your plan to work today by taking the first step.

The plans of the diligent lead surely to plenty, but those of everyone who is hasty, surely to poverty.

PROVERBS 21:5 NKJV

Spinning Wheels

Just because you have a PDA, an organizer, or a desk calendar does not mean that you are a planner. Often, people use schedules to manage their chaos. A planner does not just go from appointment to appointment because they are on his calendar. Instead, the calendar is a tool to manage his goals and plans. You may remember your grandmother telling you that haste makes waste. Without taking the time to plan your day, week, or even life, you hurriedly use up your time without accomplishing the important things that bring success.

Planning begins with a vision of your future. You can develop financial, social, professional, and spiritual goals. Once you have a goal in mind, you plan accordingly to achieve it. For example, if you want to improve your financial situation, you determine your goal. Then you determine what steps you will take to attain that financial goal. You may want to cut your spending or increase your income with a second job. Then you have a guide, or plan, to follow and keep you progressing toward your goal of attaining the financial status you desire.

> **A plan can give you direction, focus, and accountability.**

Without some type of plan, you may wander haphazardly wasting effort and time. A plan can give you direction, focus, and accountability to remain diligent in your endeavors. Avoid spinning your wheels. Maintain control of your schedule; do not let it control you.

Review your calendar. Make sure that you have evidence of your goals accounted for in your schedule. If you do not, schedule time into your day as appointments to develop them.

God did not give us a spirit that makes us afraid but a spirit of power and love and self-control.

2 TIMOTHY 1:7 NCV

Power Play

A department manager was upset with a new directive from the company president. He was so upset that he immediately called the president's office and insisted that he speak to the president at once. The secretary explained that she could not connect him at the moment due to the president's ongoing current appointment. The man became even more incensed and asked her if she realized that he was a department manager. She answered that she did know who he was. She then explained that she was only a secretary, but she was the one who connected the calls. He had authority, but she had power.

Authority is vested in a person's position. It is accepted by subordinates because it flows from the top down in the hierarchy of an organization. Many people think that authority is power or influence. But power is simply the ability to get others to do what you want them to do (or not do in the case of the manager's phone call). So anyone can have power regardless of his position.

> **Power is simply the ability to get others to do what you want them to do.**

But power can be destructive if it is not balanced with love and self-control. Getting others to do what you want does not have to be done through coercion, punishment, or authority. When power is exhibited through love, your influence on others not only accomplishes your purpose but values others.

Realize your impact on others. Exhibit a loving power that is in the best interest of those you influence. Ensure that the other person gains esteem or success through your actions.

Let the words of my mouth and the meditation of my heart be acceptable in Your sight, O Lord, my strength and my Redeemer.

Psalm 19:14 nkjv

Daily Pleasantries

You talk all day long. You talk to coworkers, customers; maybe you even mumble to yourself at times. Estimations state that an average person speaks between 125 and 250 words per minute—that is quite a few words exchanging in a single conversation. With so much communication transpiring, it is important to realize the impact of words. Your words are powerful tools to use for encouragement to others and honor to God.

Using your words cautiously may not be so easy, nor may you consider it to be the natural response, especially in difficult conversations. However, you should censor your words before they are spoken. You could see your mouth as the filter for your words. Just as a water purifier filters out unhealthy substances, your mouth can catch the toxic material of your words and dispense only the healthy portions.

You can use conversation that is good for the encouragement necessary for others to thrive in their responsibilities. Touch the lives of those around you with carefully chosen words. As you carefully choose your words with others, you will honor God by your positive display of encouragement.

> **Touch the lives of those around you with carefully chosen words.**

Sometimes a person's whole attitude can change just because a kind remark or heartfelt compliment was given to him. Sharing even simple comments of how beautiful the day is or how lovely someone looks can bring glory to God and brighten someone's day.

Check your communication filter. Dispense pure words of hope and affirmation by integrating sincere compliments and genuine appreciation in your conversations with your coworkers and clients.

The LORD is close to everyone who prays to him, to all who truly pray to him.

PSALM 145:18 NCV

Dear God

When people get to the end of their human capabilities of solving their problems, they often say, "Well, there is nothing left to do but pray." But prayer is not a last resort. God is near to you as soon as you pray. He is awaiting your request for help. He is eager to be the forerunner of your life. Prayer can be your first response to every situation. Prayer is simply a conversation with God.

Just as with a colleague, sometimes you enjoy having a special time of fellowship in a quiet setting where you can discuss important issues. But with peers, you do not always have to wait for an appointment to have a talk. You have a mutual understanding that you can make impromptu calls when you need to get advice or share excitement. For those quick conversations, you do not need a prearranged meeting. You can simply chat with your buddy on the cell phone while doing other things.

> **God is near to you as soon as you pray. He is awaiting your request for help.**

Your communication with God can be the same. Special moments of solitude and reverence may be preferred when you need more intimate time with God. But you can pray while you are holding on a phone call, driving to an appointment, or walking through the hallways at work. God does not expect an appointment. He is available for the important decisions, the small frustrations, and the celebratory announcements. He is near, listening, and ready to respond to your call.

Practice multitasking with prayer. Consider using the normally wasted waiting time in lines and at stoplights. Be creative and find three new opportunities in your day to surprise God with an impromptu prayer.

I glorified you on earth by completing down to the last detail what you assigned me to do.

JOHN 17:4 MSG

Divine To-Do List

Each day's action list holds a full day of opportunity to accomplish many things. You may even have multiple lists for your day: meetings, errands, client follow-up, family responsibilities, and so on. With so many activities to accomplish during your day, the lists can become overwhelming. When you cannot see the trees for the forest, it is time for you to prioritize.

Establishing priorities will help you accomplish the most important things first, leaving the less-needed items till the end. To properly prioritize, first determine what is important and what is just urgent. Some things are both. Important things must be addressed first. If you are not a morning person, or your schedule will not permit you to tackle the most important item at the beginning of your day, you can at least

> When you cannot see the trees for the forest, it is time for you to prioritize.

schedule it for later in the day and make it a "do not disturb" time period. Effectively organizing your daily tasks will give you a sense of accomplishment in your day.

Sometimes overlooked on the to-do list are the things that sustain you spiritually. You must know what God wants you to do with your day to truly be successful. Just like your other errands and tasks, you can schedule time for prayer, meditation, inspiration, and ministry during your day. God's items should always be assigned top priority on your daily action list.

Make an action list of your most important jobs to do for God tomorrow. Find a place in your daily schedule to place them. Make sure you assign the highest priority to God.

You are worried and upset about many things. Only one thing is important.

LUKE 10:41–42 NCV

When Plans Go Awry

Martha was exasperated. More than a dozen guests had arrived for her dinner party and she had a table to set, food to prepare, and dishes to clean. But her meal wasn't running according to plan. She was supposed to have help from her sister, Mary. But Mary was distracted and ignored her requests for help. When Martha had had enough of doing all the work alone, she finally went to the guest of honor himself, Jesus Christ. Since she couldn't get Mary to do her part, Martha enlisted his help. Jesus, however, did not respond as Martha anticipated. Instead, he gently admonished her. Mary had figured out the one thing that Martha needed to learn, which was to worship.

Worship may sound like an unusual response to problems. Worship alone may not necessarily make all your problems crumble to dust. However, worship is the most important point of your attention when facing problems. When you focus on worshiping God, you realize the many things that worry and upset you become less important. Worship refocuses you. It helps you to see problems from another perspective of eternal importance.

> **When you focus on worshiping God, you realize the many things that worry and upset you become less important.**

Like Martha, your well-planned event or project may not play out exactly as it was orchestrated. In the midst of your plan gone awry, be sure to stay focused on worship. When you concentrate on God more than the problem you are facing, it not only blesses God but builds your faith.

⁓卅♡

In stressful situations, refocus your attention on God. Ask him to provide you with wisdom and peace about the situation before you take corrective action.

Until now you have not asked for anything in my name. Ask and you will receive, so that your joy will be the fullest possible joy.

JOHN 16:24 NCV

The Winning Question

That corner store looks familiar; maybe I passed it already. Yes, that is definitely the same store. I must be driving in circles! Where is the right road? I could stop and ask for directions . . . No, I'll just loop around once more; surely I'll find it . . . You wonder why you feel compelled to continue driving when you know you are lost. It is the same impulse that urges you to continue assembling your project without reading the directions. Could it be your own sense of certainty that you know the answers that forces your tenacity? Or is it just a matter of efficiency in trying to save time? Sometimes when you continue your search or labor on your own, you do end up lost or with extra pieces left, if you even accomplish the project assembly at all.

With modern innovations such as automated navigation systems in vehicles, you do not even have to stop at the corner store to ask for directions. With the press of a button or voice activation, the promise of guidance can be accessed immediately.

You do not have to become frustrated while waiting for God's promises either. You have immediate access to answers, guidance, or anything you need by simply calling out to God through prayer. The Bible is a guidebook to every project you need to be assembled in your life. Read the instructions and ask for guidance to the promises that seem to be hiding in your life.

> You have immediate access to answers, guidance, or anything you need by simply calling out to God through prayer.

~⑭

The Bible is full of promises for a successful life. Find a promise in the Bible that you want to receive from God. Pray and ask him to provide it for you.

The LORD repay your work, and a full reward be given you by the LORD.

RUTH 2:12 NKJV

Cha-Ching!

The waitress seemed quite frustrated that she was doing most of the work serving the large party seated at the tables shared by her coworker. Her fellow waitperson had a reputation for slacking off on his share of the labor while always demanding his half of the tip. Although the tip for service was quite generous, the waitress did not feel that she was receiving her full reward for all her effort.

Often the hope of financial prosperity drives you to labor hard in the workplace, only to discover that you share the wealth with someone less industrious. A seller's real estate agent often splits his commission with the buyer's agent. Salespeople sometimes share their bonuses with their managers or associates. Business partners may receive equitable dividends regardless

> **True prosperity is the receipt of God's rewards.**

of their individual diligence and commitment to the success. Many professionals will never be paid their worth. After all, how can you put a value on saving lives, educating minds, or restoring families? Yet, firefighters, soldiers, teachers, and social workers do not earn high incomes as compared to other professionals.

If you seek to receive prosperity through only monetary rewards, you may be disappointed. True prosperity is the receipt of God's rewards. Sometimes God's blessings will come in the form of financial gain. However, God also recognizes you with intangible rewards like favor among others, a stellar reputation, a happy family, or good health. Allow God to choose your rewards, and you will have a prosperous life.

⌁⁓

Make a list of all the blessings in your life with which God has rewarded you lately. Especially remember to list the intangible rewards you have received.

The LORD is close
to everyone who
prays to him, to all
who truly pray to
him.

PSALM 145:18 NCV

After I had this vision from heaven, I obeyed it.

ACTS 26:19 NCV

Well Done

Paul, the writer of Acts, was successful because he ful-filled his purpose in life. He obeyed the vision that God had given to him. College students have long addressed the question of their purposes when choosing their majors or embarking on chosen career fields. Even among middle-aged adults, the search for purpose has driven many to career changes, lifestyle adjustments, and new avocations. Paul was able to claim success because he had been faithful to carry out the vision for his life.

The *Encarta Dictionary* gives three definitions for *purpose*. First, purpose is your reason for existence—the reason for which you were created by God. The second meaning of *purpose* is "a desired effect, goal, or intended outcome of something." Finally, *purpose* is described as "the desire or the resolve necessary to accomplish a goal."

> Even among middle-aged adults, the search for purpose has driven many to career changes, lifestyle adjustments, and new avocations.

When you understand that God created you on purpose for a purpose, you can realize the vision for your own life. Your purpose is the reason for your life from which you produce your goals. As you continually focus your goals toward your vision, you can accomplish your life vision just as Paul fulfilled his own purpose in life. Review your goals often to remind yourself of your mission in life. Your sense of purpose gives you the resolve to see your vision completed successfully.

To realize your purpose, write down the recurring ideas or dreams you have had for your life. Let your sense of fulfillment guide your next steps toward successfully completing your vision.

Do not withhold good from those who deserve it when it's in your power to help them.

PROVERBS 3:27 NLT

Share the Spotlight

Whether the final encore bow of the musical, the MVP trophy at the awards banquet, or the album of the year award, one person is often chosen to recieve the winning prize. But most of the time the individual could not have succeeded in his win alone. The musical needs a performer or technician to provide the music, the most valuable player requires a teammate to assist on the field, and the song-writer needs a vocalist to present his words to the world.

Just as a winner of a grand award needs someone to help him succeed, so a leader needs an associate. When great success occurs, the leader is often standing in the shining spotlight. After all, even if you were not directly involved in accomplishing the task, you were responsible for the team selection and delegation of those who did achieve the success. But the spotlight should be shared.

> **Recognize those people around you who faithfully contribute to achieving your goals.**

Recognize those people around you who faithfully contribute to achieving your goals. Simply give credit where credit is due. If someone compliments your new letterhead, explain that Sally chose the final ink color or that Keith designed the new logo. When others rave about the excellence of the annual banquet, credit the cooks, waitstaff, and facilities teams for their diligence and attentiveness. Shining the light on others builds up their esteem and affirms their value to you.

⌐∭⊙

Print a list of those who hold support positions on your staff. Write a sincere note of affirmation to some of the support-staff members for their contributions to your team.

Patient persistence pierces through indifference; gentle speech breaks down rigid defenses.

PROVERBS 25:15 MSG

The Wall Came Tumbling Down

As much as you try, you cannot shield the people under your leadership from disappointment, disagreements, or discouragement. As long as people work together or serve customers, there will be times when they lose their tempers, get their feelings hurt, or maybe even misunderstand motives and decisions. Painful experiences can breed anger, resentment, and apathy. Indifference and defensiveness are definite barriers to an inspiring atmosphere. So, one of the greatest challenges you face is that of motivating others to perform in spite of their personal feelings.

Reconciliation is simply bringing harmony in your organization. Before you can motivate others, first realize that apathy and defensiveness probably exist in your organization even if they are not prevalent or apparent. Being oblivious to the possibility of negativity in your workplace will not make it disappear. But you can break down these destructive walls if you use the right approach.

> **One of the greatest challenges you face is that of motivating others to perform in spite of their personal feelings.**

When you find apathy evidenced by absenteeism or lack of productivity, be persistent in sharing your goals and visions for the future. Be patient in seeing change. Attitudes are not formed or changed overnight. If you use a kind word, even when responding to criticism or judgment, you will have more success than retaliating with like emotion. As the adage goes, "You can catch more flies with honey than vinegar any day." Be sure to keep your eyes keen and your heart open to bring harmony into your workplace.

~ⅶ

Check the thermostat of your organization's harmony. Ask for honest opinions from your staff about their feelings of unity and accord. If you find indifference, conquer it with gratitude and vision.

Don't try to act important, but enjoy the company of ordinary people.

ROMANS 12:16 NLT

Common Folk

Executives, managers, line workers, and facility engineers are all the same—just people. Sometimes in the corporate world you can get caught up in the caste system of the organization. Some companies have executive boardrooms, exclusive health clubs, and even elite dining rooms. In those organizations, the coveted club key almost becomes the symbol of success and acceptance. It may also become the mark of division in relationships.

You may feel that you have arrived when you get moved to the corner office on the executive floor. It may seem that you have finally crossed over to the other side of the tracks. You have left the commoners behind to mingle with the royalty. But just because you are moving up does not mean that you have to leave old friends behind.

The opportunity of a high position affords you the chance to be a bridge among all positions of people in your

> **Allow your humility to sustain positive relationships among all the people around you.**

association. Your identity does not have to be determined by your place in the organizational chart. When you can treat the mail guy with the same respect as the vice president, you have really achieved success. As you move up the ranks, be sure to remember who you really are: a commoner with royal opportunities. Allow your humility to sustain positive relationships among all the people around you despite their positions in the organization.

~

Get to know some of your coworkers by starting a conversation with someone in another department. Do not limit your relationships. Try to meet someone new this week.

If you quit listening, dear child, and strike off on your own, you'll soon be out of your depth.

PROVERBS 19:27 MSG

In over Your Head

Many times beach lovers find that they have waded out farther into the ocean than they thought. They ignore the posted warnings and disregard the lifeguard's signal, thinking that they know their own limitations. But soon you find them bobbing up and down, waving their arms for help, once they realize that indeed they are too deep and too far out into the ocean to make their way back safely.

You may have experienced that feeling of being in over your head in the water or even in business. You didn't mean to get so carried away; you thought that you could handle the waves and undertow on your own. But self-reliance will lure you into deep waters without your even noticing. When you think that you can rely on your own ability, skill, or strength to sustain you, be warned. Eventually your body, mind, or spirit will run out of strength.

> **When you think that you can rely on your own ability, skill, or strength to sustain you, be warned.**

If you find that you are out of your depth and need a little help, rely on God. If you stay within his sight and heed his guidelines, you can protect yourself from getting in too deep. God knows just how much you can handle. He also knows how to rescue you if you slip off too far from him. Ask him to throw you a life preserver if needed. Then stay close to his counsel to ensure your security.

Determine in what areas of life you are struggling to keep your head above water. Examine some ways that you can engage your faith to rely on God for help in those situations.

A wise person gets known for insight; gracious words add to one's reputation.

PROVERBS 16:21 MSG

Seeking Popularity?

The search for popularity begins in junior high school and seemingly never ends for some people. Girls want to be the sought-after best friend, and guys seek to be admired for their bravery. Adults do not escape the lure of popularity either. Many careers require it. Popularity certainly benefits celebrities, politicians, and lobbyists. But even careers for the average Joe can benefit from popularity. Whether you are the county's highest-regarded attorney or the town's most coveted wedding planner, popularity attracts clients.

Although your reputation is not based on your popularity alone, it certainly contributes to it. Popularity comes from two sources: notoriety and acclaim. You can determine which you attain with your actions. If you build your reputation by sharing insight and kindness with others, you will gain a good reputation. When you share the wisdom that you have with others, they appreciate it. If

> **Popularity comes from two sources: notoriety and acclaim.**

you can help them and they are willing to learn, lend your knowledge. When you generously and graciously benefit others by what you have learned, they will begin to seek out your advice.

Earn your popularity through a strong and influential reputation. Your reputation is a reflection of your character. As you concentrate on developing your character with integrity and service, others will tell of your good works and build your reputation for you.

Target someone who seems to be struggling in an area in which you have knowledge. Lend your expertise to them on a gratis basis. Your investment will be returned to you by their accolades.

A **person who speaks truth is respected.**

PROVERBS 21:28 MSG

R-E-S-P-E-C-T

Although you may be granted power, you are not as easily given respect. Respect is not bestowed upon you as you attain positions of authority. You have been told that respect must be earned, not demanded. But no one gives an exact formula for earning it. You may have been told that you must prove yourself. But how you have to prove yourself may not be explained.

The way to gain respect among your peers is to continually keep your word. You may remember your grandparents using such phrases as "His word is his bond" or the "gentleman's agreement." The notion that a man's word is as sacred as a written contract is almost obsolete in today's society. Although your word may not be as highly esteemed in this era, you can increase its value.

By keeping your word as your bond, people will at least hear you out. When you have their attention, you should speak truthfully. Speaking the truth is not always easy, and it doesn't mean that you have to hurt others with unabashed honesty. Truth telling is simply speaking only what you know is true. Repeating unsubstantiated opinions or rumors about

> **The way to gain respect among your peers is to continually keep your word.**

others is not trustworthy. When you say what you mean, and you mean what you say, people may not always like your message, but they will learn to trust it. You earn respect by the proven validity and reliability of your word over time.

When you are asked your opinion of a matter, consciously decide to tell the truth. You may have to buffer it with gracious words, but speak truthfully and keep your word, and you will get respect.

For everyone to whom much is given, from him much will be required; and to whom much has been committed, of him they will ask the more.

LUKE 12:48 NKJV

A Little Dab Won't Do for a Leader

Unlike the Brylcreem that held the ducktailed hairdos in place in the 1950s, a dab of responsibility will not cover it for the leader. Leaders are responsible for decisions that affect people, processes, and profits on a daily basis—a great responsibility. With each increase in authority that you are given, your responsibility also increases. If you aspire to be a great leader, expect to accept increasing levels of responsibility.

The higher you climb in your organization, the more authority you are likely to be assigned. The privilege of exercising new authority costs an increasing amount of responsibility for the people and tasks under your supervision. Often, the visibility of your success and mistakes increases with your authority and responsibility too. The more your position is elevated in the organization, the less room you have for mistakes because of the depth and breadth of their effects. You are accountable to your organization for how well you assume your responsibility.

> **The privilege of exercising new authority costs an increasing amount of responsibility.**

The realization that other people are counting on your decisions can be sobering. But be encouraged. With increased authority and responsibility also comes the opportunity of greater influence. If you want to impact others around you, your influence is vital. Unlike hair cream, you cannot just smear a dab of responsibility here and there. Effective leaders consistently accept responsibility and exercise influence for organizational success.

Take some unsolicited initiative and volunteer for a new project or task at work. Prove yourself trustworthy of the responsibility by completing the assignment successfully.

In quietness and confidence shall be your strength.

Isaiah 30:15 NKJV

Spiritual Recess

Taking a rest seems unthinkable to some type A personalities. They ask why you would waste time doing nothing when you could be doing something. You can even spot their "If you have time to lean, you have time to clean" signs posted in their work areas. But just as rest from physical labor is required for the body, so also rest for the mind and soul is needed.

When you give thought to the word *restoration*, you find its simple definition within the word *rest*-oration. In other words, stop talking. Even the silent rehearsing of conversations does not bring restoration to your mind or soul. Many leaders complain that they cannot fall asleep at night because it takes so long to downshift the activity of their brains. Your brain processes so much information every second that you need to allow it to slow down and recharge every now and then.

> **Just as rest from physical labor is required for the body, so also is rest for the mind and soul needed.**

You can find many ways to strengthen your mind through simple silent treatments. Like some southerners, follow the example found in Britain and enjoy high tea in the afternoon. Use the time to sit quietly and listen to soothing music or sounds of nature. Take a ten-minute field trip by daydreaming about an exotic destination. Or you might even venture to have a five-minute nap in the afternoon. Give your mind and spirit some down time. You will find the recess quiet refreshing and rejuvenating.

Set your timer for five to ten minutes of quiet time in the afternoon. Refrain from reading, talking, or planning. Just listen to relaxing sounds and restore your soul.

My son, if you receive my words, and treasure my commands within you, so that you incline your ear to wisdom, and apply your heart to understanding; yes, if you cry out for discernment, and lift up your voice for understanding, if you seek her as silver, and search for her as for hidden treasures; then you will understand the fear of the LORD, and find the knowledge of God.

PROVERBS 2:1–5 NKJV

Treasure Hunt

If you were a Spielberg fan in the 1980s, you may have seen *Goonies*, the story of a group of self-proclaimed misfits searching for a lost treasure. Although the goonies were ridiculed for believing that the gold could be found, they searched diligently for the treasure. When the kids found the treasure ship full of the "rich stuff" as they called it, they were careful to leave the captain's treasure untouched. They maintained respect for the captain and a healthy fear of his warnings not to touch his personal treasure. In doing so, they were able to avoid the booby traps and later rescue their families from financial ruin with the remaining treasure that they discovered in the sunken ship.

Wisdom is the real "rich stuff" for which you should search. Insight is more valuable than gold and gems. Just as the goonies found their treasure, you can find the hidden treasure of understanding if you seek diligently. Proverbs even

> **When you seek wisdom, you will gain understanding of the power of God.**

gives a treasure map to follow. Listen to the wiser, more experienced leaders around you. Try to understand the way they think. Ask questions of them. Study diligently in the areas they suggest you need to grow as a leader.

When you seek wisdom, you will gain understanding of the power of God. Just as the goonies respected the captain, maintain a proper balance of respect and fear by heeding God's advice. He has a storehouse of treasured wisdom waiting for you to find it.

Target an area of your job in which you need more wisdom. With the help of a mentor, develop and implement an action plan to more effectively address the targeted area.

Humans are satisfied with whatever looks good; GOD probes for what is good.

PROVERBS 16:2 MSG

First Impressions

You have only ten minutes before the clients arrive at the meeting, and the room is a mess. You quickly shove papers in drawers, straighten the stacks on your desk, and rearrange the chairs around the table. When the group arrives they would never guess that just moments before your office was in disarray. You have managed to make a good first impression. Everything looks good.

But not everything that looks good is always good. There are days when you put on a smiling face and pretend that all is well, when in reality you are dealing with difficult challenges. Whether you are in the boardroom or at a church event, people may expect you to be "together" all the time. People are impressed by what appears to be good rather than what truly is good.

> **People are impressed by what appears to be good rather than what truly is good.**

God is concerned with what is in fact good to the core. God cares about how you really feel about your life, your work, and your relationship with him. He wants things to be right between you and him. Open up to God and tell him about the areas of life that frustrate or challenge you. You can be yourself with God. He isn't looking for a good first impression from you. If you are struggling with doing things the right way, he can help you. He is the One who created you and shares every moment of your life with you.

Identify your three biggest frustrations at work. After prayerful thought, list some steps for each that you can take to address the challenge.

Obedience is far better than sacrifice.

1 SAMUEL 15:22 NLT

Woe Is Me

Cell phones can be such a nuisance. It seems that wherever you go, someone's obnoxious ring or boisterous conversation can be overheard by everyone around him. Cell phone interruptions can even be heard in churches, at weddings, and at funerals, of all places. You wonder if the mandate of a cell phone makes a person feel more needed or important. The urgency of leaving a business meeting to receive a call has seemingly replaced the rudeness of entering late because one was caught on the phone with an important call. Some even have the brashness to announce the reason for the call in a martyr's tone.

When you see others arriving late to meetings or answering interruptive phone calls, it does not mean that they are more important or indispensable than you. Sacrificing your personal time, or someone else's professional time, does not equate to success. It is far better to set your phone on silent ring and respect those in the meeting with you than to take the intruding call.

> It is far better to put your phone on silent and respect those in the meeting with you than to take the intruding call.

Serving God does not have to be so sacrificial that it causes inconvenience or disruption in your life. God does not expect everyone to sacrifice to the point of woe or martyrdom. But he is interested in your obedience to him. When you pray or read your Bible, give God your full attention. You can please him by accomplishing those things that he asks of you.

⌐॥◌

Set your clock a few minutes early so that you can arrive early to meetings. Set your phone on silent ring while there so that you can give your full attention where it is due.

In quietness and
confidence shall be
your strength.

ISAIAH 30:15 NKJV

Good did not send His Son into the world to condemn the world, but that the world through Him might be saved.

JOHN 3:17 NKJV

Man with a Mission

Jesus Christ was a man with a mission. He stated that his mission was to come to earth to offer salvation to those who wanted it. Everything that Jesus did was focused toward accomplishing that mission. Jesus was a man of prayer, instruction, and encouragement, all of which led others to believe in his mission. He was able to state his mission in life to others. He made it known, with no hidden agenda.

You can follow the example of Jesus in this way. Know your mission and state it in ten to fifteen words that you can recite easily. One woman's mission statement is to "ignite others' passion for Christ," and she carries it out as a prayer leader in her church. Another woman's mission is to "help others realize their full potential." She lives it out by homeschooling her children and mentoring youth in the community. Develop your own mission statement that can be a guide to your life.

> **Teach others what you have learned in life.**

Once you are sure of your mission statement, be willing and ready to share your mission with others. Like Christ, commit your endeavors to God through prayer. Teach others what you have learned in life. Encourage them to succeed as you have succeeded. Jesus was not shy to share his mission. It was embedded in him and in those around him through his words and actions. Follow his example and live out the mission of your life.

〜〜

Share your mission in life with someone else this week. Ask them to help you stay focused on that mission as you address the various areas of responsibility in your life.

Don't use foul or abusive language. Let everything you say be good and helpful, so that your words will be an encouragement to those who hear them.

Ephesians 4:29 nlt

Around the Watercooler

Every organization has a hub for casual conversation. Whether it is the watercooler, the teachers' lounge, or the staff break room, there is likely a place where the Monday news can be heard buzzing. You may find a challenge in avoiding the hub of conversation altogether. But you can sound a different voice amid the chatter.

Unwholesome talk covers a lot of ground. You could consider negativity, rumors, gossip, and untruth to be unwholesome. Whew. You may think you have that covered, since you do not involve yourself in such destructive communication. But wait. When you read beyond the warning of what not to do, you are presented with a challenge. It is not

> **It is not enough to use self-control only to withhold unsavory conversation.**

enough to use self-control only to withhold unsavory conversation. Silence alone is not the self-control needed in the workplace. You fight against a negative with a positive. Engage yourself in the building up of others.

The challenge presented to you here is to encourage others according to their needs. Ignoring others is not an option. You are to help them by encouraging them in the areas that they need it. You are to benefit others with your words. Your voice may be a lone voice in a cloud of conversation. But your words can bring hope and inspiration to others.

⁓⟩⟩◦

Join a conversation that you would normally avoid. Infuse positive and encouraging comments in the dialogue. Meet the challenge of meeting the needs of others.

$C$are for the flock of God entrusted to you. Watch over it willingly, not grudgingly—not for what you will get out of it, but because you are eager to serve God.

1 PETER 5:2 NLT

The Servant Leader

A school principal once said that she couldn't wait for the summer to come. She explained that she could get so much more work done without the teachers and parents interrupting her all the time. Her work had become drudgery. Her job was about completing tasks and earning a paycheck, rather than helping parents and teachers make a difference in the education of children.

It is easy to fall into the trap of the daily grind. Your job can so consume you that you lose focus. Your employees and customers can rely on you to the point of your distress. If you find that you are more concerned with getting things done than affecting people, it may be time to remember the sheep. Peter gave the illustration of the shepherd caring for the sheep to remind you that others rely on you.

> **Those who are under your care expect you to protect, guide, and nurture them.**

Those who are under your care expect you to protect, guide, and nurture them. Sometimes sheep stray or bite. But it is the shepherd's responsibility to discipline them and teach them the correct way to live with the other sheep.

Think of yourself as a shepherd with your own flock. As a leader, you are called to a special purpose. You are a shepherd. You may need to nurture others to serve customers, teach them to lead coworkers, or train them to earn profits. Realize your significance to those counting on you, and lead them with care.

~ℳ⊙

Count your sheep — make a list of those who count on you for guidance and nurture. Assess your shepherding skills with each one under your care.

W̲e are His workmanship, created in Christ Jesus for good works, which God prepared beforehand that we should walk in them.

EPHESIANS 2:10 NKJV

A Real Piece of Work

If you have been searching for your identity, you have just hit the jackpot. Ephesians contains it all by telling you who you are, why you were created, when your job was planned, and what you are to do every day. First of all, you are his workmanship. That is, you are God's own design. God imagined you and created you. You were sculpted by God.

The reason you were created was to do good works. You need only determine which good works you will do. You will find your significance in what you do for others. God prepared your opportunities in advance. When you were created, God assigned opportunities to you.

> **God imagined you and created you. You were sculpted by God.**

There are no coincidences in your life. Each day is scheduled by God's plan.

You know who you are and why you were created; now you are to carry out those good works. In other words, you should look for your opportunities to do good things for others. You were specifically designed to do so; your life is significant to others. As you go throughout your day, pause frequently and observe the opportunities around you. Take advantage of the moments that you can open a door for a stranger, buy someone's lunch, or give a friend a ride home. You may be surprised at the accomplishment you feel at the end of the day.

⸻

Try to do something good for a new person every day for a week. At the end of the week, reflect on the ways that those good things affected both you and the people you blessed.

Be strong in the grace that is in Christ Jesus.

2 TIMOTHY 2:1 NKJV

Fortitude

In the '80s stepping was popular, in the '90s it was spinning, and in the new decade kickboxing and yoga have become the rage. Now many fitness experts explain that it is all about strengthening the core. By strengthening the muscles in your trunk areas you can better support your spine and movement. You can develop a strong core with concentrated movements in the midsection of your body. A strong muscular core helps all your muscles to operate in better harmony. Personal trainers assign crunches, stretches, and isometric movements to help you develop a powerful core that results in proper posture and a fit figure.

Consider your spiritual health as needing the same type of core strength. A regimen of physical exercises will not strengthen your spiritual core though. You can develop your spiritual strength by installing some simple exercises in your daily routine. Prayer is central to your spiritual well-being. Prayer is simply conversation

> **Prayer is central to your spiritual well-being.**

with God. The more you talk and listen to God, the more you will know him. Bible reading is another way to develop your strength spiritually. Read to learn and explore. Just as in physical exercise, you will discover that it energizes you to accomplish more in your day.

When you have a stable relationship with God, it pervades other areas of your life. You will find that a strong spiritual core will fortify your relationships, your peace of mind, and your worldview. Start exercising not only the body, but the soul, too.

You can combine your physical exercise with your spiritual strengthening. Try saying a simple prayer while you walk the treadmill or ride the bike this week.

M̲ost assuredly, I say to you, a servant is not greater than his master; nor is he who is sent greater than he who sent him.

JOHN 13:16 NKJV

Chain of Command

Tenure and seniority are no longer brass rings to promotions in corporations. Skill, knowledge, and social adeptness are all as important as loyalty to most of the personnel decision makers. So, there are many times when a younger, less-experienced manager may be selected instead of the more experienced associate vying for the same position. In fact, there are times when the guy with the most seniority, who feels deserving of the position, is asked to train the new hire to do the job that he thought he would have himself.

Sometimes, it is hard to submit to your boss. But face it; everyone has a boss. The president answers to the executive board, and they in turn answer to the stockholders. It is hard to find where the buck actually stops at times. There will be times when you cannot agree or do not understand the decisions that your boss makes. If your boss is also the rookie that you trained, it may even magnify the chal-

> **Even if you are wiser or more experienced, you will do well to respect the position of your boss.**

lenge. But even if you are wiser or more experienced, you will do well to respect the position of your boss.

Remember that you are no more, or less, important than your supervisor. Even if you doubt her decisions, you can be supportive by being submissive to her authority. Be the follower that you would like to lead. Offer understanding and support—even bosses need it now and then.

Ask your boss what you can do to support or assist him with an upcoming project or challenge. Then follow through with no motive except that of genuine cooperation.

May the Lord our God show us his approval and make our efforts successful. Yes, make our efforts successful!

PSALM 90:17 NLT

Success by God

Success has been defined in many ways. Earning a six-figure salary may define success for you. Building your dream home may mean success. Attaining a prestigious title may grant the feeling of achievement. You may have big ideas of what success really means. But success does not have to be a lofty goal to reach. You can experience success every day.

When you are successful, it simply means that you have achieved what you intended to do. You can attain a great sense of success by making many marks of achievement to reach while striving for the landmark moments in life. For example, if your grand goal is to own a company, set smaller goals to attain in the process. You may have a goal to select a busi-

> **As you create your agenda for the day, remember to seek God's guidance.**

ness name, another to officially incorporate, another to locate a facility or financing. As you satisfy each smaller goal, you will not only get closer to achieving your big goal, but you will experience satisfaction as well.

God will bless you as you work toward accomplishing those things that he inspires in you. In his kindness, he will help you to succeed. Commit your plans to him each day. As you create your agenda for the day, remember to seek God's guidance. He will bring the success you deserve as you diligently work toward the accomplishment of your goals.

Select a big goal that you have yet to accomplish. Break that goal into smaller, more achievable goals. As you complete each small goal, celebrate your success.

God has given gifts to each of you from his great variety of spiritual gifts. Manage them well so that God's generosity can flow through you.

1 PETER 4:10 NLT

The Gift Registry

One of the most motivational strategies that you can implement is to encourage people to use their gifts to contribute to others. Even though you realize that every person has been created with unique talents and gifts, many adults do not realize their own talents until someone else pinpoints them. You are in the privileged place of helping others discover their gifts and talents. Simply notice what others are good at doing or about what they are passionate, and you will discover where their talents lie. By sharing your observations with them, you may be able to provide the affirmation that they need to express themselves through their gifts and talents.

Once someone has discovered his gifts, offer a place for him to use them. If he is passionate about health, then put him in charge of the wellness campaign. If she has a knack for sending cards of encouragement, enlist her to send the company birthday cards each month. Even when teaming people together for projects, you can be careful to group them according to their giftings so that individual capabilities complement one another.

> **People need to see that their talents are not simply to bring them enjoyment, but to be contributed for the greater good.**

People need to see that their talents are not simply to bring them enjoyment, but to be contributed for the greater good. Gifts and talents can be shared to bring success to others. When you strengthen the individual players of the team; you strengthen the team collectively.

⁓⁗⊘

Be sure that you are aware of your own talents and contributing them. List your less-used talents and brainstorm some ways to contribute them in your workplace.

A fool's wrath is known at once, but a prudent man covers shame.

PROVERBS 12:16 NKJV

Water Off a Duck's Back

People-watching is intriguing. If you want to learn about temperance, courtesy, or patience, you have only to visit a grocery store or shopping mall during Thanksgiving week. The roadways are filled with enraged drivers, and the long lines display many impatiently tapping feet. Sometimes you can even find a little pushing and shoving to grab the final coveted turkey. But unfortunately, you do not have to wait for busy holidays to find irritated people.

Some people wear their frustration on their faces, and it resounds in their tones even at their jobs. Sometimes, you may even get caught in the cross fire of someone's dissatisfaction with a corporate policy. Try as you may, your kind smile may not be enough to ward off the sour disposition of a disenchanted customer. But you do not have to let someone else's challenge become your issue.

> **You do not have to let someone else's challenge become your issue.**

When you find yourself getting the brunt of another person's irritation, you can choose how to respond. You can retaliate by ignoring them or maybe even mirroring their behavior, but that reaction really only shows intemperance on your part as well. You can absorb the insult like a sponge and let its negative effect pervade your day. Or, you can simply let it roll off you like water off a duck's back. When you respond to an insult with kindness, you are proved to be the sensible person.

Inquire of those around you at work. If you are soaking up the frustrations of others, make a determination to shake it off and have a good day anyway.

Whenever trouble comes your way, let it be an opportunity for joy. For when your faith is tested, your endurance has a chance to grow. So let it grow, for when your endurance is fully developed, you will be strong in character and ready for anything. If you need wisdom—if you want to know what God wants you to do—ask him. . . . But when you ask him, be sure that you really expect him to answer, for a doubtful mind is as unsettled as a wave of the sea that is driven and tossed by the wind.

JAMES 1:2–6 NLT

Wisdom for the Asking

The remembrance of test-taking days in school sends chills down most spines. Entering your professional career may not bring test reprieve. Salesmen take new-product knowledge tests, and doctors complete Continuing Medical Education courses, and most other careers require some type of assessment to ensure professional standards are being kept up to par. The tough thing about tests is that you are expected to perform on your own with no help from the instructor. It is nearly impossible to remember everything that you studied, and some questions posed on the exam are difficult to interpret. Your required independence only adds to your stress.

Life also gives tests. There are times in life when you get into trouble. Sometimes your choices cause your problems for you. Often, you have no control over the problems you find yourself in. In either case, it is challenging to be glad about problems in life. But the

Thankfulness comes in passing the tests of life.

thankfulness comes in passing the tests of life. God allows difficulties to come in life to prove your faith, not only to him but to you, too.

Unlike in school and career, you can get help during life's exams. You do not have to wait until the test is over to ask for clarification or assistance. You can ask God to help you understand the lessons of life in which you are being tested. He will even give you the answers to the problems on the tests if you only ask for his wisdom.

⟨∭⟩

If you have a life test, view it as an opportunity to assess your character. Identify an area in which you see marked growth or the need for more learning.

The Lᴏʀᴅ is good to those who wait for Him, to the soul who seeks Him.

Lᴀᴍᴇɴᴛᴀᴛɪᴏɴs 3:25 ɴᴋᴊᴠ

Good and Ready

Most people spend time waiting. You may be waiting for God to bring an answer to some situation you are facing in your job, family, or ministry. Sometimes you may find yourself waiting because you propel yourself into doing so by choices that you make like declining a promotion because of the schedule requirements. Sometimes you find yourself in the waiting room due to circumstances beyond your control, like impending mergers and downsizing. Waiting can be frustrating. But waiting is the process that occurs between a promise of something and the fulfillment of it.

Waiting rooms can be places of joyful anticipation, such as when you are waiting to hear that you got the promotion. Or they can be places of fearful apprehension, like when you are waiting to hear if your position was the one cut. In either case, during the waiting you may be flooded with many emotions of excitement, fear, or nervousness.

> **Waiting is the process that occurs between a promise of something and the fulfillment of it.**

Experiencing the feelings of waiting is part of the process of trusting God's timing.

Waiting has always been a part of a life of faith. When you trust God, you learn that God's timing is not necessarily your timing and sometimes you have to wait on Him. If you try to handle things on your own, you could be missing an opportunity to learn, grow, and be blessed. God will bring the promise to pass when he feels that you are good and ready to receive it.

Dust off a dream that you shelved long ago. Make your waiting worthwhile by developing your dream in detail. When the time is right, you will be prepared to act on your plan.

The LORD said: "Surely it will be well with your remnant; surely I will cause the enemy to intercede with you in the time of adversity and in the time of affliction."

JEREMIAH 15:11 NKJV

911

Batman is sleeping in the bat cave. Superman is stuck in a phone booth. Wonder Dog cannot even be found. The movies never seem to have a problem finding rescuers for their disasters, but where is a superhero when you need one? Imagine shouting out for help when you have a financial crisis, and the Budget Buster comes with extra funds to help you. Maybe Captain Crisis could fly in and solve your problems when the machinery on the assembly line goes down. That would be an awesome way to solve your problems.

You can be rescued in times of crisis. Just as Batman stopped the Riddler, God can stop your enemies in their tracks. Maybe *enemy* is too strong a word to use. Your business competitors may not be trying to disable you with kryptonite. But there are people

> **You do not need a superhero when you have God.**

who sometimes present obstacles—either deliberately or unintentionally—in your path to success. When you have to work alongside those people for a period of time, it may feel as if you are fighting an enemy.

When you find yourself dealing with a disaster, do not distress. Never fear, help is near. You have a direct 911 line to God. He can rescue you from your crisis even faster than a speeding bullet. You do not need a superhero when you have God.

∽𝕄𝕠

Determine the biggest trial in your life right now. Call out for help. Then, list the ways that you see God rescuing you from the trial.

Trust the LORD with all your heart, and don't depend on your own understanding. Remember the LORD in all you do, and he will give you success.

PROVERBS 3:5–6 NCV

Thunderous Whisper

Airplanes and ships do not make sense. Such masses of metal staying in the air or afloat in the sea seems impossible. Yet, millions of people board them every year for business travel and long-awaited vacations. Ants and bees cannot be explained either. Their bodies should not be able to exhibit such strength. But you have witnessed bees buzzing in the air and ants carrying ten times their weight. Sometimes you cannot depend on your own understanding of how or why things work.

You cannot figure God out either. The Bible says that God knows the number of hairs on your head. He also hears every prayer that is spoken. How he can give his full attention to each person at the same time is puzzling. Sometimes you just have to trust what the Bible says about God, even if you cannot understand it.

> **Sometimes you cannot depend on your own understanding of how or why things work.**

If you listen closely, you can hear a thunderous whisper from heaven urging you to trust God more than your own reasoning. You may not see how you can have a profitable year with the losses you have sustained, but you can trust that God will supply what you need whether or not you earn the profits you had hoped. Maybe you do not understand how you will ever get the job of your dreams, but you can trust that God can connect you with the right people at the right time. Just listen to his encouraging voice. He created the bee, didn't he?

Look around you for the once-impossible things that have become possible. Encourage your faith and trust in God by giving him the credit for the possibilities in life.

Whitewashing bad people and throwing mud on good people are equally abhorrent to GOD.

PROVERBS 17:15 MSG

Mudslinging and Whitewashing

Tabloids are known for mudslinging the celebrities. Spin doctors are known for whitewashing the politicians. Most people in the real world of business have been guilty of one or the other themselves. But to consider them equally wrong may be a new consideration for you. Viewing the childhood treasure *Bambi*, you learned that "if you can't say something nice, don't say anything at all." It is no surprise that saying bad things about good people, or any people for that matter, is wrong.

Learning not to dismiss the wrongdoing of others may be harder to learn than Bambi's lesson. After all, you do not want to be the one to point out someone's flaws. You definitely do not want the job of confronting the wrongdoer. Yet this proverb encourages you to view both mudslinging and whitewashing in the same way.

Blaming the innocent for a group's failure or overlooking the guilty even in success is wrong. Although you may not be in the position of being the whistle-blower, you can at least answer questions truthfully. In a pinch, you may be asked for your opinion, and pleading the Fifth Amendment may not be an option for you. Remember to speak the truth, the whole truth, and nothing but the truth, and you may need God's help to do so.

> Speak the truth, the whole truth, and nothing but the truth.

Monitor your own comments when others begin speaking negatively about a person or dismissing injustice in your workplace. Stand for the truth by your words and actions.

M̲ake me truly happy by agreeing whole-
heartedly with each other, loving one
another, and working together with one
heart and purpose.

PHILIPPIANS 2:2 NLT

Unified Vision

Like-mindedness brings harmony and unity to your
organization. The more everyone in your work community
embraces the values and goals of the organization, the more
likely you will be successful in your endeavors. A conductor
takes several different players and inspires them to work
together to create one harmonious sound. Likewise, mold-
ing several differing opinions from a diverse work group is
key to creating unity in an organization. Like the conductor,
you begin by creating vision. Everyone in the orchestra

needs to understand what the piece will sound like when it is accomplished. Everyone in your organization needs to envision the organization's goal.

The conductor also consistently communicates the vision. After a group rehearsal, the conductor works with each section. He instructs them on how to perfect their contribution to the performance. Even within each section, some of the individual players may need specific direction or encouragement.

> **Everyone in your organization needs to envision the organization's goal.**

Finally, the conductor and leader alike compel others to embrace the vision. The players not only understand the vision, but they become part of accomplishing the vision. Once the players realize that their part is vital to the harmony of the piece, they understand their significance. Your responsibility is to create, communicate, and compel the vision for your organization. As the unified vision is embraced, harmony will resound.

~∭

Rehearse your organization's vision in a simple explanation. Find new ways to make the vision fresh and compelling. Share it with others in your organization as inspiration for unity.

Cynics look high and low for wisdom—
and never find it; the open-minded find it
right on their doorstep!

PROVERBS 14:6 MSG

Door-to-Door Wisdom

You have searched in every nook and cranny for your keys. After fifteen minutes and three people helping you, they are found right on your desk in the most obvious place. You never even thought to look on your desk. You were sure you would have noticed them before in such an obvious spot. Sometimes things are so apparent that they stare you in the face and you just overlook them.

Wisdom is required for you to be successful in leading your organization. Leaders are always seeking answers to questions and solutions to problems. Sometimes the answers to your questions are right before you and you just do not recognize their value. When you are searching for a new staff person, look at the obvious candidates within your organization. When you are trying to trim the budget, seek counsel from those with inside working knowledge of your company. More than likely, the employees know where time and product are wasted better than an outside consultant would know. Be sure to look in the obvious places for the answers and solutions you are seeking to resolve.

> **Sometimes the answers to your questions are right before you.**

Sometimes you need a reminder that you can trust those around you to guide you and assist you in your leadership. By looking in the most obvious places and keeping an open mind to suggestions made by your own organization's experts, you may find that wisdom is all around you.

Identify an issue you have been trying to resolve on your own. Ask coworkers to share their expertise about the issue. Propose a change and negotiate the resolution within the organization regarding the issue.

Remember the LORD in all you do, and he will give you success.

PROVERBS 3:6 NCV